Lecture Notes in Economics and Mathematical Systems

Managing Editors: M. Beckmann and W. Krelle

245

Jochen E. M. Wilhelm

Arbitrage Theory

Introductory Lectures on Arbitrage-Based Financial Asset Pricing

Springer-Verlag Berlin Heidelberg GmbH

Author

Prof. Dr. Jochen E. M. Wilhelm
Lehrstuhl für Betriebswirtschaftslehre
mit Schwerpunkt Finanzierung an der Universität Passau
Postfach 2540, D-8390 Passau, FRG

ISBN 978-3-540-15241-5 ISBN 978-3-642-50094-7 (eBook)
DOI 10.1007/978-3-642-50094-7

Softcover reprint of the hardcover 1st edition 1985

PREFACE

The present 'Introductory Lectures on Arbitrage-based Financial Asset Pricing' are a first attempt to give a comprehensive presentation of Arbitrage Theory in a discrete time framework (by the way: all the results given in these lectures apply to a continuous time framework but, probably, in continuous time we could achieve stronger results - of course at the price of stronger assumptions). It has been turned out in the last few years that capital market theory as derived and evolved from the capital asset pricing model (CAPM) in the middle sixties, can, to an astonishing extent, be based on arbitrage arguments only, rather than on mean-variance preferences of investors. On the other hand, arbitrage arguments provided access to a wider range of results which could not be obtained by standard CAPM-methods, e.g. the valuation of contingent claims (derivative assets) or the investigation of futures prices.

To some extent the presentation will loosely follow historical lines. A selected set of capital asset pricing models will be derived according to their historical progress and their increasing complexity as well. It will be seen that they all share common structural properties. After having made this observation the presentation will become an axiomatical one: it will be stated in precise terms what arbitrage is about and what the consequences are if markets do not allow for risk-free arbitrage opportunities. The presentation will partly be accompanied by an illustrating example: two-state option pricing. After having presented the theory - which in turn will confirm the structural properties of CAPM-related models - there will be given some selected applications which can well be read in advance in order to provide some intuitive background for the formal parts of the theory. It seems worthwhile to mention that Arbitrage Theory as understood in these lectures has (almost) nothing to do with the Arbitrage Pricing Theory as developed by ROSS (1976, 1977). Some remarks on the existing weak relationship between the two will be made in the section containing the applications.

A first draft of these Lecture Notes has been real lecture notes which the author produced (and handed out to a small but interested group of students) during his stay at the Institute of Operations Research, Department of Economics of the University of Aarhus(Denmark) in the late

1983. It is a pleasant duty to express my gratitude to J.A. Nielsen who invited me, to his family and colleagues for the warm reception I experienced there and for the stimulating discussions on various topics we had.

Bonn, West Germany, April 1985

TABLE OF CONTENTS

0. INTRODUCTION 1

1. THE LINEAR STRUCTURE OF CAPITAL ASSET PRICING MODELS 3

1.1. THE BASIC IDEA OF THEORIES OF FINANCIAL ASSET PRICES. 3

1.2. CASH-FLOW ANALYSIS 5

1.3. THE CLASSICAL CAPM 6

1.3.1. Some Assumptions and Notations 6

1.3.2. Mean-Variance Efficiency 9

1.3.3. The Valuation Formula and Related Issues 14

1.3.4. The CAPM Structure of Asset Returns 18

1.3.5. Synopsis of Results in the CAPM Theory 19

1.4. THE CAPM-VERSION BY BLACK 20

1.4.1. The Derivation of Valuation Formulas 20

1.4.2. The Structure of Asset Returns in BLACK's Model. 24

1.5. THE CAPM-VERSION WITH NON-MARKETABLE INCOME 25

1.5.1. The Derivation of Valuation Formulas 25

1.5.2. The Individual Portfolio Structure 28

1.6. THE SEGMENTED MARKETS MODEL 31

1.7. SYNOPSIS OF THE MAIN RESULTS 35

1.8. THE ROLE ARBITRAGE PLAYED IN THE DESCRIBED ASSET PRICING THEORIES 36

2. TAXONOMY OF ARBITRAGE IN FINANCIAL MARKETS 40

3. MODELLING AND FIRST CONSEQUENCES OF ARBITRAGE AND NO-ARBITRAGE CONDITIONS 43

3.1. NOTATIONAL CONVENTIONS; ARBITRATION AND SPREADS 43

3.2. ARBITRATION AND NO SPREADS: RESULTS WITHOUT TRANSACTION COSTS 45

3.3. FREE LUNCHES 50

3.3.1. Concepts and Definitions 50

3.3.2. Transaction Costs and Free Lunches 54

0. INTRODUCTION

It is one of the most natural economic 'laws' that one and the same good or commodity should sell, at the same time, at only one price, provided that transaction costs and cost of transportation are negligible. This is the essential in JEVONS's 'Law of Indifference' (JEVONS (1871)). The reason why it is so natural is that, otherwise, there would be an incentive to buy at the low and to sell at the high price coming up with a riskless *arbitrage* profit. This operation - buying at the low and, simultaneously, selling at the high - sometimes is called a 'spread'. If we speak of a *risky* spread - in contrast to the riskless spread just described - in case there is time or transportation or even processing to go between a purchase and a sale, then most economic activity consists of risky spreads: a bank collects short term funds to make long term loans facing the risk of rising interest rates; a dealer buys lots of commodities to resell them in later periods facing the risk of a weak demand or of an aggressive competitor; a producer buys raw materials, employs workers and machines to produce and to sell goods facing the risk of decreasing prices or changing tastes. In sum, risky spreads are the heart of any economic activity at all, the existence of rikless spreads, however, should be considered as a temporary abnormity.

The present lectures deal with markets where such abnormities are absent: we will study formal conditions which preclude riskless arbitrage opportunities to exist and will analyse consequences thereof. Our main concern is with financial asset markets though some of the results would be valid in a more general framework. Arbitrage considerations in financial markets have brought forth at least two very prominent classical results: the Interest Rate Parity Theory of foreign exchange rates (KEYNES (1923)) and the Theorem on the Irrelevance of the Capital Structure of the Firm (MODIGLIANI/MILLER (1958)). In the more recent past, arbitrage arguments lead to a fruitful theory of option pricing (BLACK/SCHOLES (1973), COX/ROSS/RUBINSTEIN (1979)). In what follows it will be shown how a general theory of financial asset pricing can be based on the assumption that risklessarbitrage opportunities - in a sense to be made clear - do not exist. The mode of procedure, however, will be the other way round: in Section 1 we will present some well-known one-period models of capital asset pricing in order to highlight the fact that they all share a common linear structure of asset prices. It will be seen that this structure is a consequence of more or less explicitly stated assumptions on the non-existence of riskless arbitrage opportunities. Section 2 provides a taxonomy of arbitrage in financial markets followed by a discussion in Section 3 how arbitrage operations can be modeled, with and without a consideration of transaction costs. Section 4 contains the precise statement of so-called 'no-arbitrage conditions' which mean conditions that guarantee the absence of riskless arbitrage opportunities. This section additionally contains the consequences which no-arbitrage conditions have for the structure of asset *prices*. In Section 5 it will be seen that no-arbitrage conditions imply very appealing properties for the structure of asset *returns* and a nice correspondance to the concept of mean-variance efficiency, a concept which, for a long time, has been the heart of capital asset pricing models. A final Section 6 will end our discussion with some selected applications. A list of assumptions and a list of symbols which are in varying use are available at the end of the text just before the references.

1. THE LINEAR STRUCTURE OF CAPITAL ASSET PRICING MODELS

Arbitrage Theory has turned out to be a fundamental tool in analysing financial markets and financial decisions. Financial decision making benefits from Arbitrage Theory by the concept of valuation by arbitrage. Loosely speaking, valuation by arbitrage enables us to reveal existing riskless arbitrage opportunities in cases a choice has to be made among two or more financial decision alternatives. The underlying concept will be explained at a later stage. Arbitrage Theory itself is concerned with the analysis of financial markets and theories thereof. It can be seen as a theoretical basis of any reasonable theory of financial asset prices. The following introduction is to show that all the capital asset pricing models advanced in the literature - we will, of course, consider a sample only - share a common structural property. At a later stage we will see that this common property can be deduced from a very simple model of those financial markets which do not provide risk-free arbitrage opportunities.

1.1. THE BASIC IDEA OF THEORIES OF FINANCIAL ASSET PRICES

Let us first have a look on what is the basic idea in constructing theories of financial asset prices. In sciences which are concerned with real world phenomena, a theory is to explain or, even better, is to predict events or instances which take place in the real world given certain side or boundary conditions. A theory of financial asset pricing has to start from the empirical observation that financial assets (stocks, bonds, convertibles, options etc.) yield prices at certain points in time at certain market places. So we have on the empirical level, formally spoken, a correspondance which associates to each financial asset its market price(s) (look at the upper part of Figure 1).

Any theory of financial asset pricing now aspires to uncover characteristics of financial assets which *explain their prices*. Formally, such a theory attempts to construct a mapping which associates to any bundle of characteristics of financial assets its theoretically derived price; this mapping is conveniently called a *price functional*

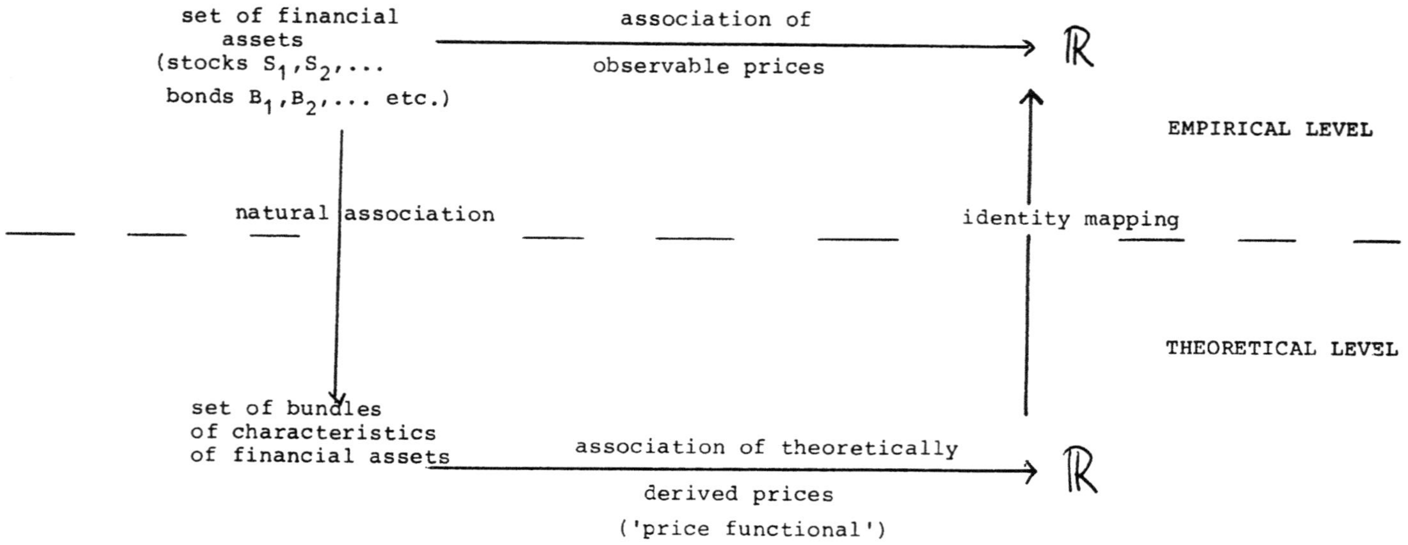

FIGURE 1: The basic idea of financial asset pricing theories

(look at the lower part of Figure 1). The price functional and, thus, the whole theory therefore includes two basic elements: the choice of an appropriate set of characteristics and the derivation of the price functional. The theory has explanatory power with respect to real world asset prices if the structure presented in Figure 1 can be completed to be a commutative diagram, i.e. running in the upper part from left to the right hand side, first, yields the same real number (price) as going down first, running over to the right hand side in the lower part then, and, finally, climbing up along the arrow at the right hand side.

1.2. CASH-FLOW ANALYSIS

We are now prepared to have a look on concrete financial (or capital) asset pricing models. In order to exemplify the elements of the diagram presented in Figure 1 we first will rely on a very simple kind of asset pricing model: cash-flow analysis. By means of cash-flow analytic techniques the value of a project is measured by the sum of its discounted cash-flows. If we apply this concept to financial asset pricing we arrive at the typical present value formula. In terms of Figure 1: the characteristics of financial assets to be chosen for that 'theory' are the future dividends, coupon payments etc. which accrue to the owner of the asset (look at Figure 2). Given the interest rate r we get for the theoretically predicted price P_0 of stock S_1 which promises future dividends (assumed for sure) $d_1, d_2, d_3, \ldots$:

$$P_0 = \sum_{j=1}^{T} (1+r)^{-j} d_j$$

It should be well noticed that, in this first example, *the price of any asset is a linear functional of its dividend stream.* This is an important feature which will be repeatedly observed in the following. Another instance, however, is remarkable: in this example we took dividends (or more generally: the cash payments) of a stock (financial asset) as the relevant characteristic and adopted the present value formula as exogeneously given; there was no deeper theoretical argument from which we derived present value as a price functional. In a later section it will be seen that Arbitrage Theory can provide the missing theoretical basis.

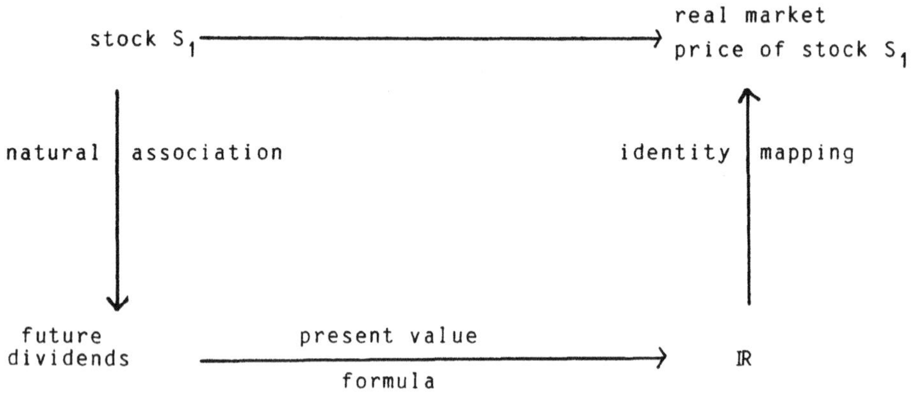

FIGURE 2: The basic structure of present value theory

1.3. THE CLASSICAL CAPM

1.3.1. Some Assumptions and Notations

Our second example comes closer to modern capital market theory. Within the model to be presented now, the *characteristics* as well as the *price functional* will be endogeneously derived from deeper theoretical arguments. The Capital Asset Pricing Model (CAPM) developed by SHARPE (1964), LINTNER (1965) and MOSSIN (1966) starts from several assumptions on the market and from some further assumptions on individual behavior in the market. The assumptions on the market are usually comprised in saying that markets are frictionless (no transaction costs, no taxes, no problems caused by indivisibilities or short sales restrictions). In addition a risk-free asset is assumed to exist. The assumptions on the individual investor consist of the following three:

- no exogeneously given income
- investors plan mean-variance efficient end-of-period wealth positions

- investors share common beliefs on the first two moments (expectation and variance) of the distribution of every feasible end-of-period wealth position ("homogeneous beliefs").

Given these assumptions the end-of-period wealth of an arbitrary investor can be written as follows:

$$w = P_1x + (1+r)x^o \qquad (1)$$

where

w end-of-period wealth

P_1 vector of end-of-period asset prices (cum dividend)

P_1x inner product of the vector random variable P_1 and the ordinary vector x

x portfolio of risky assets

r rate of return on the riskless asset

x^o initial wealth invested in the riskless asset.

The set of feasible end-of-period wealth positions is constrained by the investor's budget:

$$w_o = P_ox + x^o \qquad (2)$$

where

w_o initial wealth

P_o vector of asset prices (ex dividend) at point in time 0

P_ox inner product of vector P_o and vector x .

We now take the opportunity to introduce some concepts which will be frequently used in the sequel; to some extent they correspond to the empirical and the theoretical level, respectively, of financial asset pricing as conceptualized in Figure 1. We introduce the *portfolio space* X_p to be the set of all possible portfolios (x^o,x)

which consist of the risklessly investet amount of initial wealth x^0 and the (physical) portfolio of risky assets x . The assumptions on the market imply that the portfolio space is, in fact, a *real linear space*. The *budget plane* as given by the budget constraint (2) consists of all portfolios (elements of X_p) which meet (2) given a certain initial wealth w_o; the budget plane clearly is a hyperplane in X_p.

Another valuable concept will be introduced by the set X of all possible (uncertain) end-of-period wealth positions which can be achieved by the construction of appropriate portfolios from X_p . This set X will be called the *return space*; in fact, the assumption on the market imply that X is a *real linear space* (of random variables). We are now able to define two fundamental linear mappings:

$$c \; : \; X_p \longrightarrow \mathbb{R}$$ *'cost functional'*

and

$$L \; : \; X_p \longrightarrow X$$ *'end-of-period wealth operator'* or, more frequently, *'return operator'*

(Mnemotechnically, L is to remind us of the fact that $L(x^0,x)$ is the liquidation value of portfolio (x^0,x) when liquidated at the end of the period in question)

The definitions are:

$$c(x^0,x) \; = \; P_0 x + x^0$$

$$L(x^0,x) \; = \; w \; = \; P_1 x + (1+r)x^0$$

One should have in mind that L is an isomorphism if the end-of-period prices $P_1^1,\dots,P_1^n$ of risky assets are stochastically linearly independent (if all variances exist this is the case if and only if the covariance matrix $C = COV(P_1, P_1)$ is non-singular; note that we use COV if at least one argument is a vector of random variables; cov will be reserved for the covariance of two scalar-valued random variables): $L(x^0,x) = 0$ implies that $P_1 x$ is non-random; hence x must be zero because P_1 is a vector of stochastically linearly independent random variables. But, $L(x^0,x) = 0 = P_1x + (1+r)x^0 = (1+r)x^0$ implies $x^0 = 0$ if $r \neq -1$ holds which we will assume throughout.

1.3.2. Mean-Variance Efficiency

Returning to the derivation of the CAPM we introduce the precise notion of a *mean-variance efficient* (in the sequel often simply *efficient*) portfolio. To any portfolio (x^0,x) we define a three-dimensional vector $G(x^0,x)$ in the following way:

$$G(x^0,x) = \begin{pmatrix} -\ c(x^0,x) \\ E(L(x^0,x)) \\ -\ var(L(x^0,x)) \end{pmatrix}$$

$G(x^0,x)$ reflects the costs, the expected value and the variance of the end-of-period wealth associated with the portfolio (x^0,x).

DEFINITION 1: Using the usual vector notation we say that (x^0,x) *dominates* (y^0,y) if $G(x^0,x) \geq G(y^0,y)$ holds. We say that (x^0,x) *strictly dominates* (y^0,y) if the former dominates the latter and $G(x^0,x) \neq G(y^0,y)$ holds.

Clearly: a certain portfolio dominates another one if it does not require more initial wealth to be established, its expected end-of-period wealth is not smaller and its variance is not greater than that of the other one. It strictly dominates another one if at least one of these inequalities is a strict one.

DEFINITION 2: A *portfolio* is said to be *efficient* if there is no strictly dominating portfolio. An *end-of-period wealth position* is called *efficient* if there is an efficient portfolio which generates the position in question, i.e. the return of which is the position under consideration.

We can now state a first simple result:

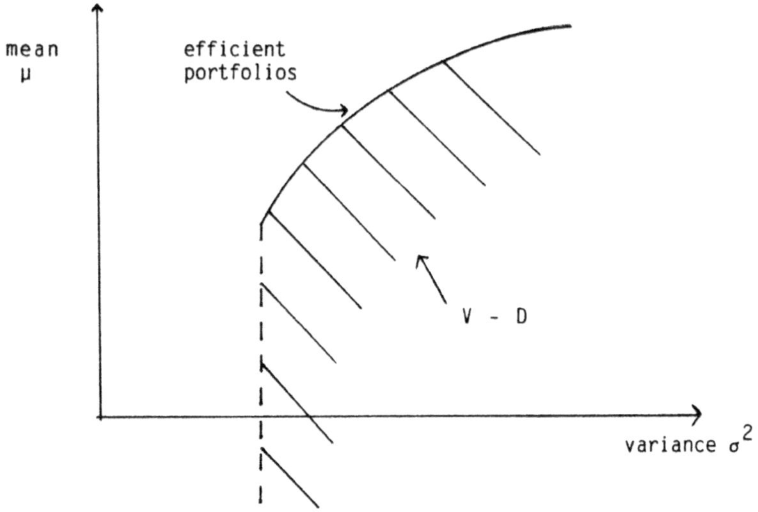

FIGURE 3: The mean-variance representation of portfolios

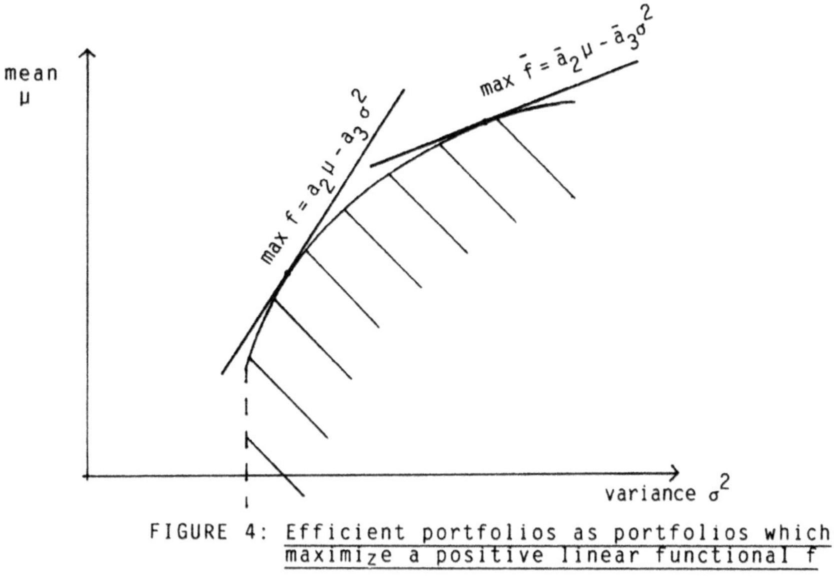

FIGURE 4: Efficient portfolios as portfolios which maximize a positive linear functional f

PROOF: The second statement is clear because the hyperplane f would not be a hyperplane at all if all the coefficients were zero. To prove the non-negativity we show that f must be a strictly positive functional, i.e. $d^+ \in D^+$ implies $f(d^+) > 0$. To see this consider $f[G(x^0,x) + d^+]$ which must not be smaller than $f(G(x^0,x))$ as we know from Proposition 1. From the linearity of f we conclude by $f(G(x^0,x)) + f(d^+) = f[G(x^0,x) + d^+] \geq f(G(x^0,x))$ that $f(d^+) \geq 0$ must be true. But $f(d^+) = 0$ would imply $f = 0$ which is impossible; hence, $f(d^+) > 0$ must hold.

The above-mentioned maximization problem requires an efficient portfolio (x^0,x) to obey the following well-known necessary conditions:

$$-a_1 + a_2(1+r) = 0 \qquad (3)$$

$$-a_1 P_0 + a_2 E(P_1) - 2a_3 Cx = 0 \qquad (4)$$

Substituting (3) into (4) yields:

$$a_2\{E(P_1) - (1+r)P_0\} = 2a_3 Cx \qquad (5)$$

The following is the central assumption of the CAPM (ROLL (1977)):

There exists an efficient portfolio (x^0,x) with $x \neq 0$. (A1)

Under (A1) condition (5) is met for some non-negative real numbers a_2 and a_3. Suppose first $a_3 = 0$. Then we get $a_2 = 0$ or, otherwise, $E(P_1) - (1+r)P_0 = 0$. The latter case is the uninteresting case of *risk neutral pricing*:

$$P_0 = \frac{1}{1+r} E(P_1)$$

This case will be excluded by assumption:

No risk-neutral pricing, i.e. $E(P_1) \neq (1+r)P_0$. (A2)

In consequence, under (A1) and (A2) the equation $a_3 = 0$ implies $a_2 = 0$ and, by (3) $a_1 = 0$ which is impossible as we know from the corollary to Proposition 1. Hence, (A1) and (A2) together enforce

a_3 to be a positive real number. We therefore may rewrite (5) to

$$Cx = a\{E(P_1) - (1+r)P_0\} \tag{6}$$

for some non-negative real number a. If a = 0 is true we can conclude from(5) that the variance of portfolio x which is xCx is zero, i.e. the end-of-period wealth of the efficient portfolio would be riskless. This will be of interest somewhere below.

1.3.3. The Valuation Formula and Related Issues

A last assumption is necessary to derive the CAPM really:

> The markets for risky assets are in equilibrium and the market portfolio x_M of all outstanding risky assets has a non-zero variance, i.e. the market's end-of-period wealth is risky at least to some extent. (A3)

Under (A1), (A2) and (A3) and the general assumptions we made at the beginning of Section 1.3.1. we get from (6) by aggregating over all individual investors

$$Cx_M = a_M\{E(P_1) - (1+r)P_0\}, \tag{7}$$

where a_M is the sum of all individual parameters a corresponding to (6). Additionally, we can conclude from (A3) $Cx_M \neq 0$ and therefore

$$a_M \neq 0\ ,\ \text{i.e. } a_M > 0 \tag{8}$$

and, thus, (6) holds for at least one investor with a = 0 .

From (7) we now get the familiar CAPM valuation formula

$$\begin{aligned} P_0 &= \frac{1}{1+r}\{E(P_1) - a_M^{-1} Cx_M\} \qquad (9) \\ &= \frac{1}{1+r}\{E(P_1) - a_M^{-1} \operatorname{COV}(P_1, P_1 x_M)\} \\ &= \frac{1}{1+r}\{E(P_1) - a_M^{-1} \operatorname{COV}(P_1, w_M)\} \end{aligned}$$

where w_M is the end-of-period wealth of the market portfolio of risky assets (simply referred to as the market's end-of-period wealth). If we introduce the market's initial wealth w_M^o in the same way we see by an easy calculation:

$$a_M^{-1} = \frac{E(w_M) - (1+r)w_M^o}{var(w_M)} \tag{10}$$

which is positive as we know by (8). a_M^{-1} is the *expected market risk premium in units of the market's variance*, sometimes called the *market price of risk*.

Using this notation we can rewrite (9) to:

$$P_o = \frac{1}{1+r}\left\{E(P_1) - \frac{E(w_M) - (1+r)w_M^o}{var(w_M)} COV(P_1, w_M)\right\} \tag{11}$$

From (11) we see very clearly that the relevant characteristic of assets for the CAPM theory of financial asset pricing is the end-of-period wealth of financial assets (P_1). In addition it is seen that asset prices are *linearly related* to these characteristics. The latter property of asset prices within the CAPM will be even more obvious in the following transformation of (11):

$$P_o = E(q \cdot P_1) \quad \text{or} \quad c(x^o, x) = E(q \cdot L(x^o, x)) \tag{12}$$

where

$$q = \frac{1}{1+r}\left\{1 - a_M^{-1}(w_M - E(w_M))\right\}$$

holds.

The price of a financial asset is by (12) given as its *expected discounted end-of-period wealth*. The discounting factor q reflects the fact that wealth is worth the more the more the market as a whole fails to supply wealth. This becomes apparent from the fact that q takes on a high value in case the market's end-of-period wealth w_M is poor (below its average) and that q is low in case the market's end-of-period wealth is well above its average. In a sense, the deviation of all-over market wealth from its average may be interpreted as a *scarcity indicator* for the price system. We will see that every asset pricing theory provides its specific scarcity indicator.

Those readers who are more familiar with the CAPM in its rate-of-return form will be served by the following transformation: Divide (11) on both sides by P_0 (componentwise, of course); denote by R the vector of rates of return of the assets in question and by $\underline{\underline{1}}$ the vector whose components equal 1, then we get

$$\underline{\underline{1}} = \frac{1}{1+r}\left\{\underline{\underline{1}} + E(R) - \frac{E(w_M) - (1+r)w_M^o}{var(w_M)} COV(R, w_M)\right\} \tag{11a}$$

A rearrangement yields

$$E(R) - r \cdot \underline{\underline{1}} = \frac{E(w_M) - (1+r)w_M^o}{var(w_M)} COV(R, w_M) \tag{11b}$$

The coefficient of the covariance term of the right-hand side of (11b) can be written as

$$\frac{E\left(\frac{w_M}{w_M^o}\right) - (1+r)}{w_M^o \, var\left(\frac{w_M}{w_M^o}\right)}$$

If R_M denotes the rate of return on the market portfolio we finally get the familiar CAPM formula in its rate-of-return form:

$$E(R) - r \cdot \underline{\underline{1}} = \frac{E(R_M) - r}{var(R_M)} COV(R, R_M) \tag{11c}$$

Obviously, (11) and (11c) are equivalent as long as prices P_0 and w_M^o are non-zero; since we cannot guarantee that *a priori* , (11) is the theoretically preferable version of asset pricing models.

As a last remark we highlight the important formal feature of (12) which consists in describing asset prices as a *linear functional of end-of-period wealth positions*. BEJA (1971) was probably the first who observed and used this important structural property.

There is another interesting issue; for the moment we make an additional assumption which is a standard assumption for introductory texts on capital asset pricing:

The covariance matrix C of risky assets is non-singular. (A4)

Under (A4) consider condition (6). All efficient portfolios which contain risky assets at all ($x \neq 0$) share a common structure: they all are proportional to

$$C^{-1}\{E(P_1) - (1+r)P_0\}$$

even if there is no equilibrium. Thus, under (A1), (A2) and (A4) there is an efficient portfolio whose end-of-period wealth excess over its average may serve as the scarcity indicator of the price system. To see this simply assume a non-zero efficient portfolio $\bar{x}$ be given such that (6) (with $\bar{a}$) holds and rewrite (6) to

$$P_0 = \frac{1}{1+r}\{E(P_1) - \bar{a}^{-1}\,COV(P_1, P_1\bar{x})\} \tag{13}$$

From (13) it is easy to see that a representation (like (12)) is possible with

$$c(x^0, x) = E(\bar{q}L(x^0, x))$$

and

$$\bar{q} = \frac{1}{1+r}\{1 - \bar{a}^{-1}(P_1\bar{x} - E(P_1\bar{x}))\}$$

Remark that this result crucially depends on the non-singularity of the covariance matrix. We will see later that this seemingly technical assumption in fact has to do with arbitrage arguments. We will see that we may relax (A4) to the assumption that there is an efficient portfolio which solves (6) for a non-zero a.

1.3.4. The CAPM Structure of Asset Returns

A last observation shall end our discussion of the CAPM. The return space X consisting of all possible end-of-period wealth positions which can be generated by forming portfolios is spanned by $P_1^1,\dots,P_1^n$ the end-of-period wealth characteristics of the assets. We assume (A1), (A2) and (A4) and, thus, know that there is a non-zero efficient portfolio $\bar{x}$ with end-of-period wealth $\bar{w} = P_1\bar{x}$. From the theory of linear spaces we know that there is an appropriate subspace N such that the following direct sum decomposition holds:

$$X = [\,\bar{w}\,] \oplus N$$

where $[\bar{w}]$ is the one-dimensional linear subspace of X which is generated by $\bar{w}$. Given $\bar{w}$ we therefore have to any financial asset i a unique representation of its end-of-period wealth P_1^i in the following form:

$$P_1^i = \beta_i\bar{w} + n_i \tag{14}$$

where $\beta_i \in \mathbb{R}$ and $n_i \in N$ are uniquely determined. More general, every possible end-of-period wealth position $w \in X$ has a unique representation:

$$w = \beta_w\bar{w} + n_w \tag{14a}$$

(14) and (14a), respectively, can be transformed so that two uncorrelated additive components appear:

$$P_1^i = [\beta_i + \frac{\operatorname{cov}(\bar{w},n_i)}{(\operatorname{var}(\bar{w})}]\,\bar{w} + [\,n_i - \frac{\operatorname{cov}(\bar{w},n_i)}{\operatorname{var}(\bar{w})}\,\bar{w}\,] \tag{15}$$

It is easily seen that in fact $\bar{w}$ and the second bracket term in (15) have zero covariance. By (15) we just arrived at a decomposition of asset returns into one component which is proportional to the end-of-period wealth of the efficient portfolio which determines the price functional, and another component which is uncorrelated to the first.

From the pricing equation (13) it is immediately seen that the second component in (15) does not have any risk-influence on asset prices, it only helps to determine asset prices through its expected value. This is well understood when we now show that this component can be completely diversified away i.e. that it disappears for an efficient portfolio. From the last subsection we know that, under the conditions we have, every non-zero efficient portfolio is proportional to $\bar{x}$. Let $h\bar{x}$ be such a non-zero efficient portfolio with end-of-period wealth w . Then from (14a) we know

$$w = \beta_w \bar{w} + n_w$$

On the other hand $w = L(h\bar{x}) = hL(\bar{x}) = h\bar{w}$ must hold. From the uniqueness of the respective representation we conclude $n_w = 0$ and $h = \beta_w$ which completes our proof. The first term in (15) will be called the *systematic*, the second term the *unsystematic* one.

1.3.5. Synopsis of Results in the CAPM Theory

Given frictionless markets, a risk-free asset and investors who plan mean-variance efficient end-of-period wealth positions with homogeneous beliefs, without exogeneous income we have seen that

- asset prices can be described by a linear price functional defined on end-of-period wealth if there is an efficient portfolio of risky assets;
- in equilibrium the price functional is determined by the interest rate and the end-of-period wealth of the market portfolio of risky assets;
- if the covariance matrix is non-singular that
  - -- all efficient portfolios of risky assets have the same structure (in equilibrium or not)
  - -- the price functional is determined by the interest rate and the end-of-period wealth of any efficient portfolio (in equilibrium or not)
  - -- every end-of-period wealth position can be broken down in a systematic and an unsystematic component, the unsystematic one being diversifiable (in equilibrium or not)

-- the unsystematic component does not have risk-influence on asset prices (in equilibrium or not).

1.4. THE CAPM-VERSION BY BLACK

1.4.1. The Derivation of Valuation Formulas

BLACK (1972) gave the first substantial alteration of the CAPM. He gave up the assumption that there exists a riskless asset. If one retains the remaining assumptions stated in Section 1.3.1. one gets, with slightly adjusted notations, that efficient portfolios must meet

$$-a_1P_0 + a_2E(P_1) - 2a_3Cx = 0 \tag{4}$$

with non-negative real numbers a_1, a_2, a_3 which cannot be zero simultaneously. We adjust the assumption that no risk-neutral pricing should obtain (A2) by assuming $a_1P_0 \neq a_2E(P_1)$. In addition we suppose (A4), i.e. non-singularity of the covariance matrix; in consequence it is not possible to create a risk-free end-of-period wealth position. From these assumption we directly conclude that any efficient portfolio $\bar{x} \neq 0$ must be of the form:

$$\bar{x} = \bar{a}_2C^{-1}E(P_1) - \bar{a}_1C^{-1}P_0 \tag{16}$$

for some non-negative real numbers $\bar{a}_1$, $\bar{a}_2$. Thus, non-zero efficient portfolios are linear combinations of two specific portfolios ('funds'); one of them, $C^{-1}E(P_1)$, corresponds to the expectation operator while the other one, $C^{-1}P_0$, corresponds to the current price system, i.e. to the cost functional. This property will be found again in a more general framework (Section 5.2. below).

Adding assumption (A1) we find for the prices of financial assets:

$$\bar{a}_1P_0 = \bar{a}_2E(P_1) - C\bar{x} \tag{17}$$

Now take an arbitrary portfolio y (the end-of-period wealth of) which is uncorrelated to (the one of) $\bar{x}$, i.e. $cov(P_1y,P_1\bar{x})$ =

$= y\mathrm{COV}(P_1,P_1)\bar{x} = yC\bar{x} = 0$. From (17) we get

$$\bar{a}_1 P_0 y = \bar{a}_2 E(P_1) y \tag{18}$$

From (A1) and (4) we know that $\bar{a}_1$ and $\bar{a}_2$ cannot be zero simultaneously. If we assume - as BLACK implicitly does because he considers rates of return rather than absolute prices - $P_0 y \neq 0$ and, hence, $\bar{a}_2 \neq 0$ we see that

$$\bar{a}_1 / \bar{a}_2 = E(P_1)y / P_0 y$$

must hold. The term on the right-hand side is one plus the expected rate of return on portfolio y and, as we see, must be the same for all portfolios which require a non-zero investment and are uncorrelated to the efficient portfolio $\bar{x}$.

In the sequel it is assumed that $\bar{a}_1 \neq 0$ holds; this is the case if any portfolio which is uncorrelated to the efficient portfolio $\bar{x}$ and which requires a non-zero investment has a non-zero expected end-of-period wealth. If we introduce R as the expected gross rate of return to all such portfolios requiring non-zero investment and being uncorrelated to $\bar{x}$, and if we denote by $\bar{w} = P_1\bar{x}$ the end-of-period wealth of the efficient portfolio $\bar{x}$, then (17) may be rewritten to yield:

$$P_0 = \frac{1}{R}\{E(P_1) - \bar{a}_2^{-1}\mathrm{COV}(P_1,\bar{w})\} \tag{19}$$

which corresponds to (13) in an obvious way.

It could be asked whether there always exists such a portfolio y. Such a portfolio can be found, e.g., by minimizing the variance of y subject to the constraint $yC\bar{x} = 0$ (no correlation with $\bar{x}$) and $P_0 y = w_y^0$ (non-zero investment). A solution is given by

$$y = \frac{1}{2}\{\lambda_0 C^{-1} P_0 + \lambda_1 \bar{x}\}$$

where λ_0, λ_1 must solve

$$\lambda_o P_o \bar{x} + \lambda_1 \mathrm{var}(P_1 \bar{x}) = 0$$

$$\lambda_o P_o C^{-1} P_o + \lambda_1 P_o \bar{x} = 2w_y^o$$

for the investment w_o^y .

Since the variance of $\bar{x}$: $\mathrm{var}(P_1\bar{x})$ cannot be zero (the covariance matrix was assumed non-singular, and $\bar{x} \neq 0$) we get

$$\lambda_1 = -\frac{P_o\bar{x}}{\mathrm{var}(P_1\bar{x})}\lambda_o$$

and

$$\lambda_o \left(P_o C^{-1} P_o - \frac{(P_o\bar{x})^2}{\mathrm{var}(P_1\bar{x})} \right) = 2w_y^o$$

We now see that such a portfolio y exists if

$$P_o C^{-1} P_o \neq \frac{(P_o\bar{x})^2}{\mathrm{var}(P_1\bar{x})} = \begin{cases} 0 \quad \text{for } P_o\bar{x} = 0 \\ [\mathrm{var}(R_{\bar{x}})]^{-1} \text{ for } P_o\bar{x} \neq 0 \end{cases} \qquad (18a)$$

holds where $R_{\bar{x}}$ is the rate of return on the efficient portfolio $\bar{x}$. We only can say that this condition is violated if the 'funds' $C^{-1}E(P_1)$ and $C^{-1}P_o$ are <u>not</u> linearly independent, i.e. if there is a kind of risk-neutral pricing $P_o = aE(P_1)$ for some non-zero a; in such a case we have

$$\bar{x} = b\, C^{-1} P_o$$

for some b 0 . We find

$$(P_o\bar{x})^2 = b^2 (P_o C^{-1} P_o)^2$$

and

$$\mathrm{var}(P_1\bar{x}) = b^2 (P_o C^{-1} P_o)$$

and , hence,

$$P_o C^{-1} P_o = \frac{(P_o \bar{x})^2}{var(P_1 \bar{x})} .$$

A sufficient condition for (18a) to hold cannot be given here, but it is worthwhile to mention that there are no such difficulties if a zero-investment is admissible, i.e. $w_y^o = 0$.

If we adopt the equilibrium assumption (A3) we obtain (13) in its equilibrium form:

$$\bar{a}_1^M P_o = \bar{a}_2^M E(P_1) - Cx_M \tag{20}$$

A portfolio which requires a non-zero investment and which is uncorrelated to the market portfolio x_M is called a *zero-beta portfolio*. In equilibrium R is the expected gross rate of return on any zero-beta portfolio and (19) reads

$$P_o = \frac{1}{R} \{E(P_1) - (\bar{a}_2^M)^{-1} COV(P_1, w_M) \} \tag{21}$$

We can therefore conclude that the structure of asset prices is just the same as in the original CAPM:

- Without equilibrium the excess of end-of-period wealth of any non-zero efficient portfolio over its average serves as the scarcity indicator for the price system;
- in equilibrium the excess of the market's end-of-period wealth over its average is the appropriate scarcity indicator;
- the expected rate of return on zero-beta portfolios plays the role of the riskless rate of interest in the CAPM;
- in either case, the asset prices can be described by a linear price functional.

The only substantial difference consists of the different structure of efficient portfolios of risky assets. While the CAPM predicts all individuals to hold portfolios of the same structure this is not the case with BLACK's version; here efficient portfolios are subjectively determined linear combinations of two, under (A2) linearly independent portfolios. This fact has consequences for the structure of asset returns.

1.4.2. The Structure of Asset Returns in BLACK's Model

From the previous section we have an efficient portfolio $\bar{x}$ with end-of-period wealth $\bar{w}$ and an uncorrelated portfolio y with end-of-period wealth w_y. Thus, there is a direct sum decomposition of the return space X given by

$$X = [w_y] \oplus [\bar{w}] \oplus N$$

with an appropriate subspace N of X. For each end-of-period wealth position w one accordingly gets a unique representation:

$$w = a_w w_y + \beta_w \bar{w} + n_w \qquad (22)$$

with real numbers a_w and β_w and $n_w \in N$. Since there is no riskless asset and since the covariance matrix is non-singular we have $var(w) \neq 0$ for every end-of-period wealth $w \in X$ except for $w = 0$. Accordingly, (22) can be rewritten as follows:

$$w = [a_w + \frac{cov(w_y, n_w)}{var(w_y)}] w_y + [\beta_w + \frac{cov(\bar{w}, n_w)}{var(\bar{w})}] \bar{w} + \qquad (23)$$

$$+ [n_w - \frac{cov(w_y, n_w)}{var(w_y)} w_y - \frac{cov(\bar{w}, n_w)}{var(\bar{w})} \bar{w}]$$

By (23) any end-of-period wealth position is broken down into three mutually uncorrelated components. From this and from (19) it is clear that only the second component has any risk-influence on the price of w because it is only the covariance with $\bar{w}$ that counts. We now show that the third component is, again, diversifiable, i.e. the third component vanishes if w is an efficient end-of-period wealth position.

To prove this assertion fix the two funds $z_1 = C^{-1}E(P_1)$ and $z_2 = C^{-1}P_0$ and recall that y is a uniquely determined linear combination of z_1 and z_2, say $y = az_1 + bz_2$. Furtheron recall that the return operator L is an isomorphism because the covariance matrix is assumed non-singular (Section 1.3.1.). Let now w be efficient; then we know from (16) that

$$w = L(a^1 z_1 + a^2 z_2) = a^1 L(z_1) + a^2 L(z_2) \qquad (24)$$

must hold. On the other hand we know from (22) that

$$w = a_w w_y + \beta_w \bar{w} + n_w$$

and, therefore, by (16)

$$w = a_w L(az_1 + bz_2) + \beta_w L(\bar{a}_2 z_1 - \bar{a}_1 z_2) + n_w \qquad (25)$$

$$= (a_w a + \beta_w \bar{a}_2)\, L(z_1) + (a_w b - \beta_w \bar{a}_1)\, L(z_2) + n_w$$

must be true. Comparing (24) and (25) and recalling that we have

$$[w_y] \oplus [\bar{w}] = [L(z_1)] \oplus [L(z_2)] \quad ,$$

it is seen that $n_w = 0$ must hold which proves our assertion.

To state our results more explicitly we can say that

- all efficient portfolios can be constructed as linear combinations of two specific portfolios (in equilibrium or not); one of these portfolios corresponds to the expectation operator the other one to the cost functional;
- every end-of-period wealth position can be broken down in two systematic and one unsystematic component, the unsystematic one being diversifiable (in equilibrium or not);
- the unsystematic component does not have risk-influence on asset prices (in equilibrium or not).

1.5. THE CAPM-VERSION WITH NON-MARKETABLE INCOME

1.5.1. The Derivation of Valuation Formulas

Another attempt to cope with the unsatisfactory prediction of all investors to hold the same portfolio structure was made by MAYERS (1972) with extensions by BRITO (1977). In this version the assumption is given up that all the income an investor receives stems from perfectly liquid investment opportunities. In reality, every economic agent is expected to own some other sources of income which he cannot sell because they are not marketable or not divisible, or which he refuses to sell without explicit rational reasoning. The practically most important example may be income from 'human capital'.

If we retain the other assumptions of the CAPM and if we denote by h the income from non-marketable assets to be received at the end of the period, we see that

$$w = P_1 x + (1+r)x^0 + h$$

holds. The variance of the individual end-of-period wealth is now given by

$$\mathrm{var}(w) = xCx + 2\mathrm{COV}(P_1,h)x + \mathrm{var}(h)$$

and is, of course a convex function of (x^0,x). So Lemma 1 and Proposition 1 apply here, too. But now we have carefully to distinguish efficient portfolios and efficient end-of-period wealth positions of individual investors. We continue to use $L(x^0,x)$ for the end-of-period wealth of the portfolio of marketable assets,so that

$$w = L(x^0,x) + h$$

holds. Efficient portfolios are then defined in the same way as before by the fact that for an efficient portfolio

$$G(x^0,x) = \begin{pmatrix} -c(x^0,x) \\ E(L(x^0,x)) \\ -\mathrm{var}(L(x^0,x)) \end{pmatrix}$$

must not be strictly dominated by any feasible portfolio. If we define

$$G_h(x^0,x) = \begin{pmatrix} -c(x^0,x) \\ E(L(x^0,x) + h) \\ -\mathrm{var}(L(x^0,x) + h) \end{pmatrix}$$

then we can define efficient individual end-of-period wealth positions in an analogous way by dominance arguments with reference to

G_h. Clearly, Lemma 1 and Proposition 1 apply, both, to G and to G_h. The return space is again X, the *individual return space* is h + X which is not a linear space unless h belongs to X. Of course, realizing an efficient portfolio not necessarily gives rise to an efficient individual wealth position because of the exogeneous pre-disposed income.

As in the original CAPM we make assumptions (A1) and (A2) to arrive at

$$C\bar{x} = \bar{a}\{E(P_1) - (1+r)P_o\} \qquad (6)$$

for some non-negative number $\bar{a}$ and an efficient portfolio $\bar{x}$. Any portfolio y which generates an efficient end-of-period wealth position for a given individual investor must meet

$$a_2\{E(P_1) - (1+r)P_o\} = 2a_3\{Cy + C_h\} \qquad (5)$$

where $C_h = COV(P_1, h)$ is the vector of covariances of individual non-marketable income h with the end-of-period wealth of marketable assets. With the same reasoning as before we see that y must follow the equation (6a) which is analogous to (6):

$$Cy = \bar{a}\{E(P_1) - (1+r)P_o\} - C_h \qquad (6a)$$

We now see from (6) that if there is a non-zero efficient portfolio with a non-zero variance then

$$P_o = \frac{1}{1+r}\{E(P_1) - \bar{a}^{-1}C\bar{x}\} \qquad (13)$$

holds, i.e.

- irrespective of individual marketable income, prices can be described as a linear functional of end-of-period wealth of assets;
- irrespective of individual marketable income the excess of end-of-period wealth of an efficient portfolio over its average serves as the scarcity indicator of the price functional.

hold. Substituting these equalities into (27a) we see that total variance of an individually efficient end-of-period wealth equals:

$$\mathrm{var}(P_1 y + h) = \mathrm{var}(\hat{a}P_1\bar{x}) + \mathrm{var}(h) - C_h C^{-1} C_h \qquad (28a)$$

Equation (28a) shows that the compensating component of the individual portfolio in fact compensates for the additional risk introduced by the non-marketable income as far as possible: the first term in the right-hand side of (28a) simply is the risk any investor will face when realising an efficient portfolio. The remaining two terms reflect the residual part of the risk introduced by the non-marketable income which cannot be hegded away by the compensating component of the individual portfolio. This residual risk depends on how strong is the stochastic dependence of the non-marketable on the marketable income: if the non-marketable income can be reproduced by portfolios of marketable assets (e.g. if the market is complete) this residual risk disappears:

$h = P_1 x$ for a suitable portfolio x implies

$\mathrm{var}(h) = x C x$ and $C_h = \mathrm{COV}(P_1 h) = C x$

and, thus, $\mathrm{var}(h) = C_h C^{-1} C_h$.

It is worthwhile to mention that the residual part of total risk $\mathrm{var}(h) - C_h C^{-1} C_h$ equals the *conditional variance* of the non-marketable income, conditional on the marketable assets if all relevant random variables are jointly normally distributed. Moreover the term

$$\frac{C_h C^{-1} C_h}{\mathrm{var}(h)}$$

can be interpreted as a (generalised) correlation coefficient reflecting the (linear) stochastic dependence of the non-marketable income on marketable assets. The residual part of risk, then, reads

$$\mathrm{var}(h)\left\{1 - \frac{C_h C^{-1} C_h}{\mathrm{var}(h)}\right\} .$$

This makes very clear that the compensating component of the individual portfolio reduces the risk induced by the non-marketable income as far as the allocational power of the marketable assets allow for.

As the result of this subsection we state that

- any individual portfolio consist of a fraction of an efficient portfolio of marketable assets and an individually determined compensating portfolio;
- the individually determined compensating component hedges away the risk introduced by the investor's fixed occupational holdings as far as possible with respect to the allocational power of marketable assets;
- it is not worthwhile to investigate the structure of asset returns here because it is obviously the same as in the original CAPM.

1.6. THE SEGMENTED MARKETS MODEL

A last model will be analysed which will give another example of a linear pricing relationship. In this model a kind of market segmentation is assumed in a way which generalizes similar considerations brought about by RUBINSTEIN (1973) and LINTNER (1977). Market segmentation may appear in the reality of financial asset markets as a consequence of institutional facts or regulation . Insurance companies or investment funds may not be free to enter arbitrary segments of securities markets; as an example, investment funds in Germany are not allowed to enter the stock options market, insurance companies have and/or take only limited access to the equity markets.

In order to model such a situation we assume two distinct groups of investors A and B and three segments of the securities market. The A investors have access only to market A and to a common (+) market while the B investors have access only to the market B and to the common market (+). All three markets have no asset in common. For simplicity we assume that the A market and the B market both contain a riskless asset while the common market (+) does not.

Similar to the preceding section we have to distinguish efficient portfolios within the three market segments and efficient end-of-period wealth positions of A investors and B investors, respectively. Denoting by x^A (x^B) the portfolio held in market A (B) and by y^A (y^B) the portfolio held in the common market and introducing further indexed symbols accordingly, we get:

$$L_A(x^A, x_A^o) = P_1^A x^A + (1+r_A)x_A^o$$

$$L_B(x^B, x_B^o) = P_1^B x^B + (1+r_B)x_B^o$$

$$L_+(y) = P_1^+ y$$

and

$$w^A = L_A(x^A, x_A^o) + L_+(y^A)$$

$$w^B = L_B(x^B, x_B^o) + L_+(y^B)$$

The following abbreviations will be used in what follows (i = A,B)

$$C_i = \mathrm{COV}(P_1^i, P_1^i)$$

$$C_{i+} = \mathrm{COV}(P_1^i, P_1^+)$$

$$C_{+i} = \mathrm{COV}(P_1^+, P_1^i)$$

$$C_+ = \mathrm{COV}(P_1^+, P_1^+)$$

It is quite clear (particularly, Lemma 1 and Proposition 1 are applicable) that, under suitable assumptions, efficient portfolios in market A or B, respectively, must meet equation (6) in the following form:

$$C_i \bar{x}_i = \bar{a}^i \{ E(P_1^i) - (1+r_i)P_o^i \} \qquad i = A,B \tag{29}$$

In the same way an efficient portfolio $\bar{x}^+$ in the common market must meet (16):

$$\bar{x}^+ = \bar{a}_2 C_+^{-1} E(P_1^+) - \bar{a}_1 C_+^{-1} P_o^+ \tag{30}$$

Turning to the conditions which an efficient individual end-of-period wealth position must fulfill we see from an application of Proposition 1 and appropriate versions of (A1) and (A2):

$$C_i x^i + C_{i+} y^i = a^i \{ E(P_1^i) - (1+r_i) P_0^i \} \tag{31}$$

$$C_{+i} x^i + C_+ y^i = a^i \{ E(P_1^+) - (1+r_i) P_0^+ \} \tag{32}$$

for $i = A, B$.

A quick look on (31) reveals a strong relationship to the non-marketable assets case: $C_{+i} y^i$ is a covariance risk introduced into the market A or B by the holding of investments in the common market; these investments are non-marketable with respect to A and B markets.

The resulting covariance risk will be accounted for by transactions on the market i ; the compensating portfolio will be $-C_i^{-1} C_{i+} y^i$ which reduces the risk inseminated by the common market as far as the allocational power of i - assets allows for. On the other hand, by (32) one can see that the holdings x^i on the market i play the same role for investments in the common market. As seen from the common market, $C_{+i} x^i$ is a covariance risk which must be accounted for by transactions on the common market: $-C_+^{-1} C_{+i} x^i$ is the adequate compensating portfolio.

So, as long as no equilibrium conditions are to be observed we have by (29) and (30) exactly the same situation as in the original CAPM and the BLACK-version, respectively:

- asset prices can be described as linear functionals of end-of-period wealth of assets (in equilibrium or not);
- the excess of end-of-period wealth of an efficient portfolio (efficient within the segment in question) over its average serves as scarcity indicator of the price functional;
- the structure of individual portfolios is determined as in the case of non-marketable assets: the holdings in the specific external market play the role of non-marketable assets.

1.8. THE ROLE ARBITRAGE PLAYED IN THE DESCRIBED ASSET PRICING THEORIES

The reader may be allured to ask what the asset pricing theories described hitherto have to do with arbitrage, our main concern. The first answer is a draft on sections to follow: we shall see that the basic linear structure which we found in every asset pricing theory that we studied, can also be derived from simple arbitrage assumptions rather than from a mean-variance oriented investment behavior. Moreover, the property that asset pricing in our context is always strictly associated with mean-variance efficiency also is a consequence we can derive from simple arbitrage arguments rather than starting with it. These issues will be our concern in the next sections.

But there is another answer to be given for the role of arbitrage in the preceding derivations. This answer asserts that we have used arbitrage arguments, yet, without revealing them as such. First of all, we assigned *only one price per unit to each financial asset*. This assumption excludes riskless profits from spreads, i.e. from buying at the low and selling at the high. In addition, we assumed - frictionless markets - that a *portfolio of assets must sell for the sum of prices of its components* (technically, we assumed the cost functional to be linear). This assumption precludes further obvious riskless spreads from success. The same was assumed to be true at the end of the period: we assumed the *end-of-period wealth operator to be linear*, thereby excluding successful spreads at that point in time. But these assumptions are quite 'harmless' compared with seemingly technical assumptions we made additionally. We will now see that [(A1) and (A2)] or [(A2) and (A3)] or [(A2) and (A4)], respectively, are implicit 'no-arbitrage conditions'.

The arbitrage arguments which we revealed up to now were more or less a Law of Indifference in physical terms of assets rather than in terms of their theoretically relevant characteristics: we assumed that the current value of portfolios of assets is linear in its components and that the end-of-period wealth of portfolios, its liquidation value, is, too. Particularly, prices for portfolios obey the Law of One Price; these arguments refer, in a sense, to the empirical level of asset pricing. But if we choose a certain bundle of asset characteristics (such as dividends or future asset prices) which are expected to be theoretically relevant, we can answer the question, by definition, whether assets or portfolios are *equivalent with respect to these characteristics*; the Law of One Price has, then, an additional dimension: it is expected to apply to portfolios, too, which are equivalent in this sense.

To speak more concretely whith reference to asset pricing: if we choose end-of-period wealth of assets as the, hopefully, theoretically relevant characteristic we should expect two portfolios which realize the same end-of-period wealth - which state of the world ever occurs - to have the same current market value. In diagrammatic terms:

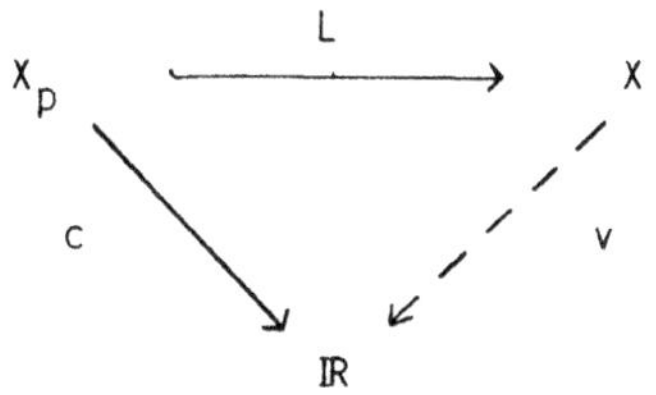

There should be a pricing functional v ('v' appealing to value) which makes the diagram commutative; a necessary condition is the Law of One Price in the sense:

$$L(x) = L(y) \quad \text{implies} \quad c(x) = c(y) \qquad \text{(LOP)}$$

If the cost functional as well as the end-of-period wealth operator is linear, (LOP) is equivalent to say:

$$L(x) = 0 \quad \text{implies} \quad c(x) = 0. \qquad (LOP_I)$$

For all our asset pricing models this is a *result* which holds under certain conditions, particularly in equilibrium [(A2) and (A3)] .
A narrower inspection shows that [(A1) and (A2)] as well as [(A2) and (A3)] and the combination [(A2) and (A4)] have always the implication that the equation

$$Cx = a\{E(P_1) - (1+r)P_0\} \qquad (6)$$

has a solution $\bar{x}$ for at least one a. In the (A4) version of the model it is additionally assumed that $\bar{x}$ can be chosen non-zero with the consequence $a \neq 0$. In this case (non-singular covariance matrix C) we immediately see that (LOP_I) holds since the end-of-period wealth operator is an isomorphism; the seemingly harmless technical assumption of the non-singularity of the covariance matrix in fact is a no-arbitrage condition:

> $L(x^0,x) = 0$ implies P_1x = const. which in turn implies $xCx = 0$ and, thus, $x = 0$ because C is non-singular, but then $x^0 = 0$ must hold, too, i.e. $(x^0,x) = 0$ and, therefore, $c(x^0,x) = 0$.

It remains to investigate cases where the covariance matrix C is allowed to be singular; this is the case if there is a non-zero portfolio z of risky assets such that $zCz = 0$ holds. If in such a case an efficient portfolio x is assumed to exist - which therefore must solve (6) (with $a \neq 0$) - then consider zCx. Because z has zero variance, z has no covariance at all, i.e. zCx must be zero. From (6) we now see

$$E(P_1)z = (1+r)P_0z \tag{39}$$

z has no variance and is, thus, a kind of hedge which duplicates the riskless asset; if such a duplicating portfolio exists the assumption of a non-zero efficient portfolio means by (39) that *the investment in such a hedge portfolio must earn the same return as the riskless asset.* This obviously implies (LOP_I):

> Assume $L(x^0,x) = 0$; then P_1x = const., i.e. x duplicates the riskless asset. By (39) we know $E(P_1)x =$ $= (1+r)P_0x$; by assumption $E(P_1)x = -(1+r)x^0$ and, thus, $c(x^0,x) = P_0x + x^0 = 0$ as long as $1+r \neq 0$ holds.

In a slightly different framework this observation is due to ROLL (1977).

It may be even more instructive to consider the case when there is no efficient portfolio of risky assets. In such a case - by the definition of efficient portfolios - there is a certain bounded variance at which arbitrarily high expected returns are possible. One should expect that to any degree of risk aversion there is the tendency to invest high amounts in such portfolios which provide enormous returns at rather low risks; such a tendency would tend to destroy equilibrium. If there is no efficient portfolio there is, in some sense, no need to balance the risk and the level of portfolio returns. The same is true if there are arbitrage opportunities. This intuitive understanding will prove right in precise terms in a later section.

We are now ready to look at the picture the other way round. Up to now we collected more or less systematically common structural properties of asset pricing theories and showed that many of the assumptions made to obtain these properties, have in fact a background of arbitrage arguments. In what follows we will develop a concise theory of what arbitrage is, how it can be modeled and what the consequences are if we assume that arbitrage is effective enough to eliminate riskless arbitrage opportunities.

2. TAXONOMY OF ARBITRAGE IN FINANCIAL MARKETS

In a later section we will formally define situations where price systems do not allow for riskless arbitrage profits. Price systems having this property will be called - somewhat misunderstandable, but in accordance with the literature - 'arbitrage-free'. Since the theory to be developed crucially depends on the specific nature of this definition the concept of arbitrage in the theory should refer to real world transactions or phenomena which we expect not to provide riskless profits when markets are sufficiently active and perfect. Let us, therefore, begin with a review of what usually - in daily economic custom and/or in the theoretical literature - is meant by arbitrage opportunities or transactions.

There are three market operations which usually are put in relation to arbitrage. The first and most traditional form of arbitrage is just to follow the economic principle: buy any good or commodity as cheap as possible, sell any good or commodity as expensive as possible. The term 'arbitrage' (or in a narrower sense: 'arbitration' or 'compound arbitration') originally was used for a calculation designed to determine the cheapest way of making a remittance between two countries. When three places are involved the calculation is called 'simple arbitration', when more: 'compound arbitration' (cf. keyword 'Arbitration of Exchange' in MUNN (1983)). The calculation includes various (cross) exchange rates and interest rates as well as transaction costs at various places. In generalizing this term we can say that *arbitration consists of the search for the lowest cost in achieving a certain intended financial position.*

The second market operation which in economic practice is sometimes identified with arbitrage exploits a difference in prices of the same good or commodity selling at the same time in (normally) different market places. If the difference is greater than normal it is called a 'spread', if it is smaller than normal it is called a 'back spread' (cf. keywords Backspread, Spread in MUNN (1983)). By a *spread* we mean *the transaction of simultaneously buying and selling one good or commodity when the transaction guarantees a riskless profit.*

These two operations, arbitration and spread, essentially refer to our empirical level of asset pricing: they do not involve asset characteristics and the concept of equivalent combinations of assets. The third operation which can be seen as an arbitrage operation, too, takes into account asset characteristics. It will be called a 'free lunch'. It is normally necessary to specify the point in time when the free lunch can be enjoyed. The first example is a free lunch *today:* given a set of characteristics chosen to delineate assets it is meaningful to speak of equivalent combinations of assets though these combinations may consist of *physically* different assets. It is important to note that the concept of equivalence must include that equivalent combinations of assets are equally desirable for every economic agent irrespective of his individual preferences or endowment. As an example look at option pricing where, under suitable assumptions,it is possible to combine risk-free bonds and stocks in such a way that the resulting portfolio dublicates the cash-flow generated by a stock option. Suppose there are no institutional disturbances like tax differentials then all rational investors should be indifferent between that portfolio and the option, except for the initial investment to make. Therefore, *a 'free lunch today' consists of turning from one combination of assets to another one which is equivalent but has a lower market price.* To the extent the market value of the two equivalent combinations differ the economic agent acquires additional risk-free income at the current time which he can use to have a free lunch today.

A somewhat wider range of operations is covered if the point in time where the lunch is available is not restricted to today. For this concept to define we need not only an equivalence relation for assets but even a partial ordering. Of course the partial ordering must also be in harmony with any reasonable preference relation and initial endowment. If we address this ordering by the term 'as least as much' we can characterize a wider notion of free lunches: *a 'free lunch' consists of turning from one combination of assets to another one which is less expensive and provides as least as much as the initial one or requires the same investment, provides as least as much, but is not equivalent to the initial one* (the formal concept of free lunches is due to HARRISON/KREPS (1979)).

Since our aim is to study markets where arbitrage opportunities are absent (i.e. such abnormities survive only very short periods of time) we have to make these concepts precise. This will be done in the next section. We introduce these concepts in an environment where transaction costs may occur. After having discussed the influence of transaction costs of the modelling of arbitrage operations we will assume them away for the rest of these lectures. We will do this because up to now there is no elaborated asset pricing model incorporating transaction costs. But our concern is to show that arbitrage theory is a basis for (probably) all asset pricing theories in use. An attempt has been made by GARMAN/OHLSON (1981) and WILHELM (1983) to incorporate transaction costs into Arbitrage Theory. There it is shown that a basic valuation principle can be derived imposing bounds on asset prices which are determined by transaction costs; this principle is much in the spirit of the transaction costs-free case. But the other results which relate arbitrage theory to existing asset pricing theories are not robust against the introduction of transaction costs. On the other hand, it is an open question whether transaction costs have, in reality, a measurable impact on prices of assets which is more than negligible. Note that professional arbitrageurs should have quite low direct costs per transaction and/or per dollar traded; most of their expenditures seem to be fixed.

3. MODELLING AND FIRST CONSEQUENCES OF ARBITRAGE AND NO-ARBITRAGE CONDITIONS

3.1. NOTATIONAL CONVENTIONS; ARBITRATION AND SPREADS

In order to formalize arbitrage operations we first have to introduce some notational conventions. We assume a set S of financial assets be given *which is not necessarily finite*. It will turn out more convenient to consider *changes of portfolios* rather than portfolios themselves as basic market objects. Such a portfolio change will be realized by executing some orders to buy and/or some orders to sell certain amounts of assets. So we depart from buy/sell orders (in shorthand B/S-orders) as our basic notion. To allow for transaction costs to be incorporated it is necessary to distinguish purchases and sales formally, rather than to model sales as negative purchases. So we model B/S-orders as pairs of orders; the first component refers to purchases while the second refers to sales of assets.

The first assumption we must make is the following:

> Assets are infinitely divisible, i.e. there can be any non-negative real multiple a part of a B/S-order. (A5)

Clearly, in the real world environment only finitely many different assets can be subject to a single B/S-order; so with assumption (A5) the natural mathematical model for B/S-orders is related to the *free real vector space* generated by the set of assets S. By F(S) we denote this free vector space which can be thought of as the set of all finite formal linear combinations of assets. Since purchases and sales are treated separately we use only those linear combinations which have positive coefficients. The resulting set is denoted by $F_+(S)$. Based upon this notation we define:

DEFINITION 3: A B/S-order (x,y) is a member of $F_+(S)xF_+(S)$; $x \in F_+(S)$ stands for the purchases, y stand for the sales. $\overline{X} := F_+(S)xF_+(S)$ will be called the *portfolio cone*. Of course, $\overline{X}$ is in fact a convex cone.

Empirically, to any B/S-order there are associated costs which have to be incurred if the B/S-order in question is carried out. These costs can depend on how the B/S-order will be executed. Suppose a

B/S-order (x,y) be given; let I(x,y) denote the set of all possible ways to execute B/S-order (x,y) (e.g. on different market places, through different brokers, in different packages etc.). So we can presume the *cost function* $\bar{c}$ to be of the following form:

$$\bar{c} \; : \; (x,y;i) \longrightarrow \mathbb{R}$$

where $(x,y) \in \bar{X}$ and $i \in I(x,y) \neq \emptyset$.

At this instant of time we should introduce the net physical position which emerges from a given B/S-order; this physical position is defined as the net change of an individual portfolio resulting from the execution of B/S-orders and, thus, is formally given by the difference of purchases and sales:

$$(x,y) \longrightarrow x - y$$

and is a mapping

$$\bar{X} \longrightarrow F(S) = X_p$$

$X_p = F(S)$ is now a model of the *portfolio space* as used before. The members of X_p will be referred to as *net portfolio changes*.

It is now an easy task to state what is to be understood by *arbitration*. Each economic agent who considers whether or not he should change his portfolio should evaluate the possible ways on which a certain change can be carried out. He will evaluate them according to the costs they require. Thus we define:

DEFINITION 4: By the *costs of a net portfolio change* $z \in X_p$ we understand:

$$c(z) = \inf \left\{ \sum_{j=1}^{n} \bar{c}(x^j,y^j;i_j) \mid n \in \mathbb{N}, \; z = \sum_{j=1}^{n} (x^j - y^j) \, , \; i_j \in I(x^j,y^j) \right\} \tag{40}$$

The resulting functional c is called the *cost functional* if it exists at all.

This definition is to be understood as follows: there are possibly many ways of buying and/or selling packages of assets which ultimately establish the same net change of a given portfolio. Arbitration enforces economic agents to search for the cheapest way to do it. This process is reflected in (40): all the costs of any such transaction within a series of transactions designed to achieve a net portfolio change z sum up to 'the' costs of that (possibly complicated) way to establish z. Any such series of transactions which results in z is a candidate the costs of which have to be evaluated in (40). Without further assumptions c(z) need not exist for any given net change z of portfolios. But, of course, if c(z) does not exist then there is a sequence of market transactions which all result in the same net portfolio change but incur strictly decreasing costs which are negative except for finitely many transactions. This, clearly, is highly valuable to anyone who plans to realize such a portfolio change. Effective markets does not provide for such opportunities. This will be formally excluded in the next section.

In the same logic we can state what a spread is about:

DEFINITION 5: A *spread* is given if $c(0) < 0$ holds.

The condition of a spread is met when there is a finite sequence of market operations which, as a whole, does not create any net change of portfolios but, in turn, creates a riskless inflow amounting to $-c(0)$ which can be consumed or invested, additionally.

Since the definition of free lunches is a little bit more complicated we prefer to delay it for a while and to first draw some conclusions from arbitration and spreads when there are no transaction costs. This will provide a better intuitive understanding of these concepts before we proceed.

3.2. ARBITRATION AND NO SPREADS: RESULTS WHITHOUT TRANSACTION COSTS

In this subsection we assume that transactions are free from specific transaction costs. Formally, we define:

and j. From Lemma 2 and Lemma 3 we therefore conclude $c(z) = -c(-z)$ and, analogously, $c(z') = -c(-z')$. Thus

$$c(0) \leq c(z+z') + c(-z) + c(-z')$$

$$= c(z+z') - c(z) - c(z')$$

$$< 0 \text{ by assumption.}$$

Consequently, the assumption $c(z+z') < c(z) + c(z')$ leads to a spread in contradiction to (A7) which completes our proof.

Our next step is to prove that the cost functional is homothetic with respect to rational numbers:

LEMMA 5: Under the conditions of Proposition 2 the cost functional exhibits $c(az) = ac(z)$ for any rational number a.

PROOF: Let $a = m/n$ hold where m and n are integers; since we know that $c(-z) = -c(z)$ holds we may assume that m and n are non-negative without loss of generality. Then we have

$$c(az) = c(mn^{-1}z) = c\left(\sum_{i=1}^{m} n^{-1}z\right) = c(n^{-1}z) + \ldots. + c(n^{-1}z) =$$

$$= mc(n^{-1}z) \quad .$$

On the other hand we know $nc(n^{-1}z) = \sum_{i=1}^{n} c(n^{-1}z) = c(\sum_{i=1}^{n} n^{-1}z) =$ $= c(nn^{-1}z) = c(z)$, from which we conclude $n^{-1}c(z) = c(n^{-1}z)$. Hence, $c(mn^{-1}z) = mn^{-1}c(z)$ which proves our assertion.

Lemmata 4 and 5 prove that under the conditions of Proposition 2 the cost functional is close to being a linear functional on the portfolio space. The remaining gap will be closed by the following assumption:

The cost functional is continuous with respect to every one-dimensional subspace of the portfolio space. (A8)

Of course, (A8) can only be assumed when arbitration is effective, i.e. together with (A6). We then can state a first main result in

Arbitrage Theory:

THEOREM 1: If

(i) the cost function is free of transaction costs,

(ii) arbitration is effective, i.e. (A6),

(iii) there are no spreads, i.e. (A7)

(iv) the cost functional is continuous with respect to every one-dimensional subspace of the portfolio space, i.e. (A8),

then there is a linear cost functional which assigns to each net portfolio change its uniquely determined market value.

PROOF: From Proposition 2 and Lemmata 4 and 5 it remains to show that $c(az) = ac(z)$ holds for any *real* number a. Because any real number is the limit of a Cauchy-sequence of rational numbers $(a_i \mid i=1,2,...)$ it is easily seen by continuity (A8) that $(c(a_i z) \mid i=1,2,...)$ has a limit $\lim_i c(a_i z) = c(\lim_i a_i z) =$

$c((\lim_i a_i)z)$; but $c(a_i z) = a_i c(z)$ by Lemma 5 and, hence,

$\lim_i c(a_i z) = \lim_i (a_i c(z)) = (\lim_i a_i)c(z)$ which completes our

proof.

In sum, what usually is the self-understanding starting point of any elaborated asset pricing theory: a linear cost functional, has been derived here from explicit assumptions:

- infinite divisibility of assets
- absence of transaction costs
- effective arbitration
- absence of riskless spreads
- continuity of prices.

The first and the last assumption are closely related. Continuity is only a matter of interest if assets are infinitely divisible. The divisibility assumption is not only for mathematical convenience, but is also related to arbitrage. If there would be demand for a half of an undivisible asset it would be profitable to take an intermediate position: to purchase one unit and to create two new securities; in the absence of transaction costs this operation can create a spread. In the real world there exists an institution which plays a similar role: investment funds. The no-arbitrage conditions stated above justify this divisibility assumption.Thus, essentially, the linearity of the cost functional is a consequence of effectively working arbitrage.

3.3. FREE LUNCHES

3.3.1. Concepts and Definitions

In order to conceptualize what will be called free lunches we have to analyse what an investor can get from a portfolio or a portfolio change, respectively. In a sense, we have to specify the 'return' of a portfolio, the return which is to characterize the portfolio in question in the sense of a theoretically relevant characteristic (Section 1.1.). There are three components which determine what an investor actually gets from a portfolio: the cash paid on assets when held over a certain period, the investor's decision to liquidate a position, (in part or completely), and the market prices prevailing when positions are liquidated. We assume that investors are interested in the 'consumption' of money in the present and in every future period of time. The basic objects the investors are, thus, concerned about are consumption patterns over time which will be formally defined below. In order to prepare such a definition we have to introduce our concept of uncertainty over time.

In what follows we assume a finite set of points in time to be given at which portfolio changes can be carried out and where cash is paid on assets. Note that the length of the time interval between succeeding points in time can be made arbitrarily small such that continuous trading opportunities can be obtained in the limit (for the continuous time CAPM see MERTON (1973a); for questions concerning the relevant set of portfolio strategies (discrete or continuous in time) see HARRISON/KREPS (1979), HARRISON/PLISKA (1981) and HARRISON/PLISKA (1983)). To each point in time $t = 0,1,2,...$ we associate a measure space $(E_t, \mathcal{E}_t)$ consisting of a set E_t of elementary events and a σ-algebra $\mathcal{E}_t$. By $(E,\mathcal{E})$ we mean their product.There are further measure spaces which are of particular interest because they describe "histories up to certain points in time t":

$$(E^t, \mathcal{E}^t) \ := \ \prod_{h=o}^{t} (E_h, \mathcal{E}_h)$$

$(\mathcal{E}^t | t = 0,1,2,...)$ can be seen as an increasing family of σ-subalgebras of $\mathcal{E}$ which represents the information available at point in time t; therefore the measure spaces $(E, \mathcal{E}^t)$ $(t = 0,1,2,...)$ will have meaning to us, too. We assume transition probabilities from $(E^t, \mathcal{E}^t)$ to $(E_{t+1}, \mathcal{E}_{t+1})$ to be given for $t = 0,1,2,...$ where $(E_0, \mathcal{E}_0)$ is deterministic: E_0 consists of just one element e_0. By Ionescu Tulcea's Theorem (NEVEU (1969)) we, then, know that there is a probability on $(E, \mathcal{E})$ compatible with all the transition probabilities. In most of the text we do not explicitly refer to this probability, but only consider *events with non-zero probability*; so we need not introduce a symbol for the probability measure at this stage. We are now able to define the notion of consumption patterns (over time) and a notion of dominance between them:

DEFINITION 7: A *consumption pattern* $(u_t | t \geq 0)$ is a sequence of measurable real-valued functions u_t on $(E, \mathcal{E}^t)$, i.e. $u_t(e_0, e_1, ..., e_T)$ only depends on $(e_0, ..., e_t)$ which is in short hand denoted by e^t: $u_t(e_0, ..., e_T) = u_t(e^t)$.

A consumption pattern $(u_t | t \geq 0)$ is said to (*strictly*) *dominate* a consumption pattern $(\bar{u}_t | t \geq 0)$ if $u_t \geq \bar{u}_t$ holds almost surely for all $t \geq 0$ (and $u_t > \bar{u}_t$ holds with non-zero probability for at least one point in time t). The (set of) points in time t for which $u_t > \bar{u}_t$ holds with non-zero probability (is) are called the (*set of*) *domination points*.

Obviously, the dominance relation of consumption patterns is in harmony with every reasonable individual preference relation, i.e. if one consumption pattern strictly dominates another one, then the former is strictly preferred to the latter by every reasonable economic agent; of course, if economic agents disagree on which events have zero-probability they, generally, disagree on the dominance relation; to avoid this it should be assumed that *individual beliefs are represented by equivalent probability measures* i.e. probability measures which have exactly the same sets of measure zero. We adopt

The logic behind this definition is as follows: if a free lunch is possible then it is possible by just changing the portfolio strategy to achieve in at least one period of time with non-zero probability a strictly higher consumption level while in the other points of time no loss in consumption has to be incurred. This is of course a preferable situation to anybody who owns the initial portfolio in questions.

3.3.2. Transaction Costs and Free Lunches

The definition of free lunches depends on the initial portfolio from which the consumption patterns can be generated. We now show that this dependence matters only if transaction costs are important. In order to simplify our discussion we assume, for the moment, the cash flows D_t obtained from portfolio holdings to be zero, i.e. it is only the process of market prices over time we are concerned with. We also restrict ourselves to the consideration of free lunches today; the same observations can easily be made for the remaining cases. A free lunch today is possible if there is a pair of consumption patterns with $u_t = \bar{u}_t$ for $t = 1,\ldots,T$ almost surely and $u_0 > \bar{u}_0$ where $(u_t | t = 0,\ldots,T)$ and $(\bar{u}_t | t = 0,\ldots,T)$ both belong to $U(x_0,e_0)$, i.e. are compatible with initial portfolio x_0. That means:

$$c_t(z_t,e^t) = c_t(\bar{z}_t,e^t) \qquad \text{for } t = 1,\ldots,T$$

$$c_0(z_0,e_0) < c_0(\bar{z}_0,e_0)$$

$$\sum_{t=0}^{T} z_t = \sum_{t=0}^{T} \bar{z}_t = -x_0$$

The dependence on the particular initial portfolio rests from the fact that, under transaction costs, the cost functionals are not necessarily linear. So, *even if there is a free lunch possible in the economy, it cannot be enjoyed by everyone*: only those investors who already own the correct initial portfolio before trading takes place can be sure to receive a free lunch today.

However, every investor, besides his particular initial portfolio, can be seen as owning a zero portfolio in excess. Assume now that there is a free lunch possible with respect to initial portfolio $x_o = 0$. Then there is one case in which every investor can enjoy this specific free lunch: if the dominated consumption pattern is generated by $\bar{z}_t = 0$ $(t = 0,\ldots,T)$, i.e. by a completely passive portfolio strategy. From definition we know that $c_t(\bar{z}_t, e^t) \leq 0$ must hold for all $t = 0,\ldots,T$ since no change is always possible with no costs. We therefore have for the portfolio strategy of the dominating consumption pattern:

$$c_t(z_t, e^t) \leq 0 \quad \text{for } t = 1,\ldots,T$$

$$c_o(z_o, e_o) < 0$$

$$\sum_{t=0}^{T} z_t = 0$$

Now take any consumption pattern compatible with initial portfolio x_o^*. We now show that there is a free lunch possible with respect to x_o^*. We fix $\hat{z}_t = z_t^* + z_t$. Then

$$\sum_{t=0}^{T} \hat{z}_t = \sum_{t=0}^{T} z_t^* + \sum_{t=0}^{T} z_t = -x_o^*$$

holds. On the other hand,

$$c_t(\hat{z}_t, e^t) \leq c_t(z_t^*, e^t) \; + \; c_t(z_t, e^t) \leq c_t(z_t^*, e^t) \quad (t = 1,\ldots,T)$$

$$c_o(\hat{z}_o, e_o) \leq c_o(z_o^*, e_o) \; + \; c_o(z_o, e_o) < c_o(z_o^*, e_o)$$

Hence $(\hat{u}_t | t = 0,\ldots,T)$ defined by $\hat{z}_t$ strictly dominates $(u_t^* | t = 0,\ldots,T)$ defined by z_t^* from which a free lunch is possible which has at least one dominating point at $t = 0$. This property gives rise to the following definition:

DEFINITION 10: We say that a *standard free lunch is possible* if there is possible a free lunch with respect to zero initial portfolio where the dominated consumption pattern requires no portfolio changes at all.

We have therefore just proven:

PROPOSITION 3: If there is possible a standard free lunch, then every investor, irrespective of his initial endowment, can be made better off.

If a standard free lunch is possible there is an opportunity to create consumption possibilities 'out of nothing'; over time the portfolio strategy starts from a zero position and ends with a zero position (in physical terms); but by borrowing and lending, by going short and going long cleverly exploiting price differentials, additional consumption expenditures become possible without creating additional obligations. Such a strategy is interesting for everyone and, if it exists, it is possible for everyone.

We will now show that the converse of Proposition 3 is true if the conditions of Theorem 1 are met, i.e. essentially, if arbitration is effective, if there are no spreads and if there are no transaction costs.

PROPOSITION 4: Suppose that the assumptions of Theorem 1 are fulfilled for every point in time and every future event. If there is a free lunch possible with respect to some initial portfolio x_0 then a standard free lunch is possible.

PROOF: Under the assumptions of Theorem 1 all cost functionals are linear. Let a free lunch be possible (for simplicity assume: today); we then have by definition portfolio strategies z_t and $\bar{z}_t$ such that

$$c_t(z_t, e^t) \leq c_t(\bar{z}_t, e^t) \qquad \text{for all } t = 1, \ldots, T$$

$$c_0(z_0, e_0) < c_0(\bar{z}_0, e_0)$$

$$\sum_{t=0}^{T} z_t = \sum_{t=0}^{T} \bar{z}_t = -x_0$$

Clearly, by $\hat{z}_t = z_t - \bar{z}_t$ and by the linearity of the cost functionals a standard free lunch is possible.

Propositions 3 and 4 show that standard free lunches are, in a sense, representative for all free lunches if the cost functionals are linear, i.e. if the no-arbitrage, no-transaction - costs conditions of Theorem 1 are met. The prohibition of standard free lunches will be the central argument in Arbitrage Theory.

There is a last statement on the set of consumption patterns which appeals to the linearity of the cost functionals. If the cost functionals are linear one would expect that two portfolios which stand for the same wealth before trading should provide the same opportunities to render consumption expenditures, i.e. the set of consumption patterns compatible with a given initial portfolio should only depend on its *market value* and *not* on its *structure*. This is indeed the case as Proposition 5 will show. But before stating it we have to introduce a generalization of the set of consumption patterns:

DEFINITION 11: For a given portfolio x we denote by $U(x,e^t)$ the *set of consumption patterns compatible with endowment* x *at* t *conditional on* e^t which are given by $(h = 0,\ldots,T)$

(i) $u_h(\bar{e}^h) = 0$ if $\bar{e}_\tau \neq e_\tau$ for some $\tau = 0,\ldots,\min\{t,h\}$

(ii) $u_h(e^h) = 0$ for $h < t$

(iii) $u_h(e^t,e_{t+1},\ldots,e_h) = D_h(x_h,e^h) - c_h(z_h,e^h) \geq 0$

for $t \leq h < T$

(iv) $u_T(e^t,e_{t+1},\ldots,e_T) = D_T(x_T,e^T) - c_T(z_T,e^T)$

(v) $x_h = x + \sum_{\tau=t}^{h-1} z_\tau$ for $h = t,\ldots,T+1$

(vi) $x_{T+1} = 0$

Of course, $U(x,e^t)$ generalizes $U(x_0,e_0)$ in a natural way; (i) and (ii) determine that consumption expenditures are considered only after e^t having occurred; neither before t nor on a path which does not start at e^t net cash flows emerge from the strategy in question. The conditions (iii) through (vi) are the same as in the definition of consumption patterns compatible with a certain initial endowment.

4. NO-ARBITRAGE CONDITIONS AND THE STRUCTURE OF PRICE SYSTEMS

4.1. THE LAW OF ONE PRICE

In this section we are interested in the existence and properties of price functionals. We know from Section 1.8. that it is necessary for a price functional to exist that some kind of the Law of One Price holds. We now state a version of such a law which is in fact in a way a conversion to Proposition 5:

THE LAW OF ONE PRICE: The Law of One Price is said to hold (with respect to point in time $t = 0$) if for any two portfolios $x, y \in X_p$ the equality

$$U(x,e^1) = U(y,e^1) \text{ for almost all } e^1 \in E^1$$

implies

$$c_0(x,e_0) = c_0(y,e_0) \ .$$

A definition with respect to any other point in time and conditional on a specific history emerged up to that time is analogous.

The spirit behind this definition is clear: it is assumed that trading takes place at point in time $t = 0$ after having received the cash payment $D_0(x,e_0)$ or $D_0(y,e_0)$, respectively. The prices at which trading actually takes place reflect the opportunities to consume which will accrue to the investors after trading will have been closed. These opportunities are fully described by the events e^1 and the endowment x or y, respectively, from which consumption patterns can be generated, i.e. by $U(x,e^1)$ or $U(y,e^1)$, respectively. If both opportunity sets coincide, the Law of One Price requires their initial prices to be the same.

A very simple example where the Law of One Price holds is when

$$D_1(x,e^1) + c_1(x,e^1) = D_1(y,e^1) + c_1(y,e^1) \quad \text{for almost all } e^1$$

implies $x = y$ as it is the case when within the CAPM the covariance matrix is non-singular.

For the rest of these lectures *we assume that Theorem 1 is applicable to each point in time and that the cash payments are linear with respect to portfolio holdings*. In consequence $c_t(x,e^t)$ and $D_t(x,e^t)$ are linear with respect to $x \in X_p$ for every point in time t and every event e^t. We can now redefine our *end-of-period wealth operator*

$$L_1(x)(e^1) = D_1(x,e^1) + c_1(x,e^1) \qquad \text{for } e^1 \in E^1 \text{ and } x \in X_p$$

The *return space* is given by $X_1 := L_1(X_p)$ which is a real linear space of random variables on (E,E^1) which only depend on components which belong to E_1.

We are now able to state a first simple but fundamental result:

PROPOSITION 6: If the Law of One Price holds then there is a linear price functional v_1 on X_1 which relates an asset's market value to its end-of-period wealth, i.e. for any portfolio $x \in X_p$ we have

$$c_0(x,e_0) = v_1(L_1(x)) = v_1(D_1(x,.) + c_1(x,.)) \qquad (44)$$

where v_1 is a linear functional on X_1.

PROOF: Since $D_1(x,.)$ and $c_1(x,.)$ and $c_0(x,e_0)$ are linear in x, v_1 will be linear if it is well-defined by (44). This is true if

$$D_1(x,e^1) + c_1(x,e^1) = D_1(y,e^1) + c_1(y,e^1) \text{ for almost all } e^1 \qquad (45)$$

implies $c_0(x,e_0) = c_0(y,e_0)$. From Proposition 5 we know that (45) implies $U(x,e^1) = U(y,e^1)$ for almost all e^1. The Law of One Price, then, enforces $c_0(x,e_0)$ to equal $c_0(y,e_0)$ which completes our proof.

Proposition 6 can easily be extended to more than one period after having introduced some additional notation . Let Y be the product space of Y_t $(t = 0,...,T)$ where Y_t is the space of measurable real-valued functions on (E,E^t). Hence, Y is a space of vector-valued random variables or stochastic processes. There is a subset of elements of Y which is of special interest to us; this subset spans the subspace of deterministic elements of Y and is like a basis in a

Euclidian space, it consists of

$$1_t = (0,0,\ldots,0,1,0,\ldots,0) \qquad t=0,\ldots,T$$

where the component t has value 1 while the other components are zero. Now the stream of cash payments over time which accrue to an investor who holds portfolio x over periods $h=0,\ldots,t$ can be written by

$$D^t(x) = \sum_{h=0}^{t} D_h(x,.)1_h \qquad (t=0,\ldots,T)\ ;$$

here $D^t(x)$ is a (t+1)-dimensional random variable.

We are now able to define the *t-period return operator* L^t which maps X_p, the portfolio space, into Y by the following advice:

$$L^t(x) = D^t(x) + c_t(x,.)1_t = \sum_{h=0}^{t} D_h(x,.)1_h + c_t(x,.)1_t$$

This is a natural extension of the notion of an end-of-period wealth operator. Correspondingly, we define the *t-period return space* as the image of the portfolio space under the t-period return operator. We are now in a position to state and to prove the t-period analogon to Proposition 6:

COROLLARY 1: If the Law of One Price holds for all points in time $h=1,\ldots,t-1$ then there is a linear price functional v^t on the t-period return space X^t such that for any portfolio $x \in X_p$ we have

$$c_o(x,e_o) = v^t(L^t(x))$$

PROOF: We only have to prove that $L^t(x) = L^t(y)$ implies $c_o(x,e_o) = c_o(y,e_o)$. For $t=1$ this is the content of the Law of One Price as stated above. Let the implication be true for $t=h$. Suppose $L^{h+1}(x) = L^{h+1}(y)$. This implies

$$D_{h+1}(x,.) + c_{h+1}(x,.) = D_{h+1}(y,.) + c_{h+1}(y,.)$$

By the Law of One Price as applied to point in time h we therefore conclude

$$c_h(x,.) = c_h(y,.)$$

On the other hand $L^{h+1}(x) = L^{h+1}(y)$ also implies

$$D_g(x,.) = D_g(y,.) \quad \text{for } g = 0,\dots,h$$

Hence, by our assumption the equality $L^h(x) = L^h(y)$ follows which implies $c_o(x,e_o) = c_o(y,e_o)$ which completes our proof.

With a certain topological background we can proceed a little further:

COROLLARY 2: Let Y be endowed with a topology which makes Y a locally convex topological vector space and v^t a continuous linear functional on the subspace X^t. Then there exist a continuous linear functional on Y denoted by V_t such that

$$c_o(x,e_o) = \sum_{h=1}^{t} V_t(D_h(x,.)1_h) + V_t(c_t(x,.)1_t) \tag{46}$$

holds.

PROOF: The existence of the asserted continuous linear functional is an immediate consequence of the Hahn-Banach Theorem for locally convex topological vector spaces (cf. RUDIN (1973, p. 59)): v^t can be extended to all of Y the extension being V_t. The extension is linear and continuous so that (46) holds.

REMARK: If there are only finitely many states of the world Y must be finite-dimensional; in this case the conditions of Corollary 2 are always met.

(46) is a kind of discounted cash flow result: the price of an asset (or portfolio) is determined by its 'discounted' cash payments. We are now in a position to analyse the discounted cash-flow theory under certainty. In this case Corollary 2 is applicable. We find

$$c_o(x) = \sum_{h=1}^{t} D_h(x)V_t(1_h) + c_t(x)V_t(1_t)$$

$V_t(1_h)$ is the market price of one unit of money to be safely received in point in time h. Therefore, the price of a sure asset is in fact given by the discounted cash-flows it promises. So we have derived the discounted cash-flow formula as an asset pricing theory under conditions of certainty from the Law of One Price. Remember that this pricing formula had been assumed on an ad hoc basis in Section 1.2.

4.2. FREE LUNCHES AND THE LAW OF ONE PRICE

In this section we will study the relationship between the Law of One Price and the possibility of free lunches. Intuitively, if the Law of One Price fails to hold we expect an arbitrage opportunity to exist. This intuition will be confirmed by the following proposition:

PROPOSITION 7: If no free lunches are possible today, then the Law of One Price holds.

PROOF: Assume portfolios $x, y \in X_p$ such that $U(x,e^1) = U(y,e^1)$ holds almost surely, but $c_o(x,e_o) < c_o(y,e_o)$. We choose some consumption pattern $(u_t | t \geq 0) \in U(x,e^1) = U(y,e^1)$ which is generated by x and (z_t) as well as by y and $(\hat{z}_t)$ for $t = 1,\ldots,T$. We now show that a free lunch is possible today. By taking differences we get

$$0 = D_t(x_t - y_t, e^t) - c_t(z_t - \hat{z}_t, e^t) \qquad (t = 1,\ldots,T)$$

and

$$-(x-y) = \sum_{h=1}^{T} (z_h - \hat{z}_h)$$

If we now choose $z_o^* = x - y$ (sell y and buy x) and $z_t^* = z_t - \hat{z}_t$ (adopt the portfolio strategy which relates to x) for $t = 1,\ldots,T$ we find

$$c_o(z_o^*, e_o) = c_o(x,e_o) - c_o(y,e_o) < 0$$

and

$$D(z_t^*, e^t) - c(z_t^*, e^t) = D\left(\sum_{h=0}^{t-1} z_h^*, e^t\right) - c_t(z_t - \hat{z}_t, e^t)$$

$$= D\left(\sum_{h=1}^{t-1} (z_h - \hat{z}_h) + (x-y), e^t\right) - c_t(z_t - \hat{z}_t, e^t)$$

$$= D(x_t - y_t, e^t) - c_t(z_t - \hat{z}_t, e^t)$$

$$= 0 \quad \text{for } t = 1,\dots,T.$$

Finally,

$$\sum_{t=0}^{T} z_t^* = \sum_{t=1}^{T} (z_t - \hat{z}_t) + (x-y) = 0$$

In sum we showed that a free lunch is possible today which contradicts our assumption and completes, thus, our proof.

COROLLARY: If standard free lunches are not possible which have domination points up to t-1, then Corollary 1 of Proposition 6 holds. If in addition the topological assumptions of Corollary 2 hold we even get (46).

PROOF: The proof rests on Proposition 7 and Corollaries 1 and 2 of Proposition 6. Suppose the Law of One Price does not hold at point in time h with non-zero probability. In the same way as in the proof of Proposition 7 one can see that a standard free lunch as seen from h conditional on e^h is possible where the events e^h have non-zero probability. This results in a standard free lunch with domination point h.

This Corollary can be seen as the basic result of the whole Theory of Arbitrage. It states that under quite weak conditions on the absence of arbitrage opportunities (no spreads, effective arbitration, no transaction costs, no standard free lunches) asset prices can be explained as linear functionals of their cash payments. The rest of the Theory is concerned with continuity and, thus, with Corollary 2 of Proposition 6 and resulting structural properties of the linear functionals V_t and the connection with mean-variance efficiency.

4.3. VALUATION BY ARBITRAGE

4.3.1. The General Concept

We are now able to explain what valuation by arbitrage means; if there is a certain cash-flow pattern over time one can ask for its value.

Of course, there is no problem at all if the particular cash-flow characterizes an asset which is traded on the market: its value is its market value. But what happens if the cash flow is not traded, i.e. if there is no market price to observe? Then, the concept of valuation by arbitrage searches for an object that *is* traded and exhibits the same cash-flow pattern over time. Now, the Law of One Price allows to predict the market value of the cash flow in question in case it *was* traded. If there is no portfolio (strategy) which exhibits the same cash flow pattern then every valuation is compatible with the Law of One Price.

To be precise let be given a cash-flow $d = (d_t | t \geq 0)$ which is to be valued by arbitrage. Since we assume that markets are open after the investors having received current cash flows we may suppose that $d_o = 0$ holds. In the following we are interested in the behavior of the price system when d is treated as if it was marketed. To this end we formally enlarge the set S of assets to the set S_d by means of $S_d = S \cup \{d\}$. The resulting portfolio space is given by

$$X_{pd} = X_p \oplus [d] ,$$

where [d] is the one-dimensional real linear space generated by d. As a last notational convention we distinct cash-flows $d(e^t)$ derived from d *conditional on certain events* e^t by

(i) $\bar{d}_\tau(\cdot) = 0 \quad$ for $\tau < t$

(ii) $\bar{d}_\tau(e^t, e_{t+1}, \ldots, e_\tau) = d_\tau(e^t, e_{t+1}, \ldots, e_\tau) \quad$ for $\tau \geq t$

(iii) $\bar{d}_\tau(\bar{e}^t, e_{t+1}, \ldots, e_\tau) = 0 \quad$ for $\tau \geq \tau$ and $\bar{e}^t \neq e^t$

(iv) $d(e^t) = (d_o, \bar{d}_1, \bar{d}_2, \ldots, \bar{d}_T)$

$d(e^t)$ coincides with d for every history (path) which contains e^t and equals zero otherwise; $d(e^t)$ is designed to be a member of $U(x, e^t)$ for some portfolio x of marketed assets. This property is used in the following definition.

DEFINITION 12: The cash-flow d is said to be *valued by arbitrage* if there are numbers $c_t(d, e^t)$ for every point in time $t = 0, \ldots, T-1$ and every history e^t such that the Law on One Price holds for each point in time $t = 0, \ldots, T-1$ with respect to the enlarged portfolio space X_{pd} when $c_t(d,e^t)$ is seen as the price per unit of d sold at t conditional on e^t. Particularly, if there is a portfolio x such that $d(e^1) \in U(x,e^1)$ for almost every event e^1, then we have $c_0(d,e_0) = c_0(x,e_0)$ where $U(x,e^1)$ is generated by portfolio changes in X_p only.

The definition is understood as follows: to the cash-flow which has not yet been traded we associate prices such that the resulting model obeys the Law of One Price.

We can now prove that every cash-flow pattern which results from an admissible portfolio strategy can be valued by arbitrage if within the original model the Law of One Price holds.

PROPOSITION 8: Let x be a portfolio and $d(e^1) \in U(x,e^1)$ for almost every e^1. Let the Law of One Price hold for $t = 0,\dots,T-1$. Then d can be valued by arbitrage.

PROOF: We know from assumption that $d_t(e^t) = D_t(x_t,e^t) - c_t(z_t,e^t)$ holds with

$\sum_{h=0}^{t-1} z_h = x_t$ and $e^t = (e^1,e_2,\dots,e_t)$. We define $c_t(d,e^t) =$

$= c(x_{t+1},e^t) = c(x_t+z_t,e^t)$ and $c_0(d,e_0) = c_0(x,e_0)$. It is easily seen that this definition does not depend on the particular x chosen (see Proposition 5 and the Law of One Price). It remains to show that the Law of One Price holds for every point in time $t = 0,\dots,T-1$ within the enlarged portfolio space X_{pd}. To prove this take two portfolios $y + ad$ and $y'+a'd$ at e^{T-1} and suppose

$D_T(y+ad,e^{T-1},e_T) = D_T(y'+a'd,e^{T-1},e_T)$ for almost all e_T.

We know that $D_T(d,e^T) = D_T(x_T,e^T)$ must hold for $e^T = (e^{T-1},e_T)$.

We, therefore get

$D_T(y+ad,e^T) = D_T(y,e^T) + aD_T(x_T,e^T)$

and

$D_T(y'+a'd,e^T) = D_T(y',e^T) + a'D_T(x_T,e^T)$.

By the linearity of D_T we find

$$D_T(y+ax_T,e^T) = D_T(y'+a'x_T,e^T)$$

where $y+ax_T$ and $y'+ax_T$ both belong to the original portfolio space; thus, the Law of One Price applies to result in

$$c_{T-1}(y+ax_T,e^{T-1}) = c_{T-1}(y'+a'x_T,e^{T-1})$$

and, hence, our assertion proves right for the last period. The rest of the proof is by induction together with the use of Proposition 5.

Proposition 8 has a useful corollary:

COROLLARY: Under the conditions of Proposition 8 the linear price functional as given by Corollary 1 to Proposition 6 (v^T defined on X^T) can uniquely be extended to a linear price functional $\bar{v}^T$ on $X^T \oplus [d]$.

PROOF: A member of $X^T \oplus [d]$ is uniquely defined by u + ad where u belongs to X^T and a is some real number. By Proposition 8 we can value d by arbitrage: $c_o(d,e_o) = c_o(x,e_o)$ for a suitably chosen portfolio x. Now define

$$\bar{v}^T(i+ad) = v^T(u) + ac_o(x) .$$

Clearly, $\bar{v}^T$ is a linear price functional on $X^T \oplus [d]$ which extends v^T. From the uniqueness of u+ad we get that $\bar{v}^T$ is uniquely determined, too.

4.3.2. An Example: Two-state Option Pricing

In order to further elucidate the concepts in question let us consider two-state option pricing as advanced by COX/ROSS/RUBINSTEIN (1979). In this model all the sets of elementary events equal $E_1 = E_2 = \dots = E_T = \{0,1\}$. We consider a stock, a riskless one-period asset and a European call option on the stock with excise price B. The stock price either changes by u per cent ('up') or by d per cent ('down') in each period of time where $d < u$ holds. We now show how the option can be valued by arbitrage in this model under the assumption that the stock does not pay any dividends before the option expires. Assuming that the option expires at T we know that the cash paid on the option is given by $C_T = f(s_T) = \max(s_T-B,0)$ in point in time T (and zero elsewhere) where s_T is the stock price at T. We have now to construct a portfolio x_T held over period (T-1,T] the end-of-period wealth of which equals that of the option $f(s_T)$. Let x_T^1 be the number of stocks in x_T and x_T^2 the number of riskless one-period bonds which pay 1 unit of money per bond at T. Then we must have:

$$x_T^1 s_T + x_T^2 = f(s_T) \quad ,$$

which yields two equations because there are two possible outcomes for the stock price as perceived from T-1 and e^{T-1} :

$$x_T^1 u s_{T-1} + x_T^2 = f(us_{T-1})$$

and

$$x_T^1 d s_{T-1} + x_T^2 = f(ds_{T-1})$$

The solution is:

$$x_T^1 = \frac{f(us_{T-1}) - f(ds_{T-1})}{(u-d)s_{T-1}}$$

and

$$x_T^2 = \frac{uf(ds_{T-1}) - df(us_{T-1})}{u - d}$$

Hence, the arbitrage value of the option at point in time T-1 is given by:

$$C_{T-1}(s_{T-1}) = \frac{f(us_{T-1})(1-db_{T-1}) - f(ds_{T-1})(1-ub_{T-1})}{u - d} \tag{47}$$

where b_{T-1} is the bond price at T-1 .

In order to value the option two periods back at T-2 we have to construct a portfolio x_{T-1} which has wealth C_{T-1} when held over period (T-2,T-1]. This is possible if and only if the bond price b_{T-1} is determined as soon as s_{T-1} has been realized (to be us_{T-2} or ds_{T-2}), i.e. bond prices do not introduce additional uncertainty beyond that generated by the stock price.The simplest case is when bond prices are non-stochastic or even simpler: constant over time.

A quick look on (47) shows that C_{T-1} has then two possible values if s_{T-2} is given. Then the same procedure as before leads to the portfolio x_{T-1} :

$$x^1_{T-1} = \frac{C_{T-1}(us_{T-2}) - C_{T-1}(ds_{T-2})}{(u-d)s_{T-2}}$$

and

$$x^2_{T-1} = \frac{uC_{T-1}(ds_{T-2}) - dC_{T-1}(us_{T-2})}{u-d}$$

Now denote $p = \frac{1-db_{T-1}}{u-d}$ and $q = \frac{ub_{T-1}-1}{u-d}$; then we have

$$C_{T-1}(s_{T-1}) = pf(us_{T-1}) + qf(ds_{T-1})$$

and find $C_{T-2}(s_{T-2}) = pC_{T-1}(us_{T-2}) + qC_{T-1}(ds_{T-2})$

$$= p^2f(u^2s_{T-2}) + 2pqf(uds_{T-2}) + q^2f(d^2s_{T-2}) .$$

By induction one proves

$$C_o(s_o) = \sum_{t=1}^{T} \binom{T}{t} p^t q^{T-t} f(u^t d^{T-t} s_o) \quad (48)$$

which is the two-state option pricing formula generalized to any claim contingent on the stock price s_T at T. Of course, (48) reminds to the expectation of a binomially distributed random variable if p and q can be interpreted as probabilities. This is an important feature which will be addressed again in a subsequent section.

The same example can be treated within our framework of linear price functionals. For any given e^{T-1} we know that there is a linear price functional $v_T(.,e^{T-1})$ which values end-of-period wealths by:

$$s_{T-1}(e^{T-1}) = v_T(s_T,e^{T-1})$$

and

$$b_{T-1} = v_T(1,e^{T-1})$$

But given e^{T-1} there are only two possible outcomes at T: $(e^{T-1},0)$ or $(e^{T-1},1)$. From this we see that $v_T(.,e^{T-1})$ must be of the form:

$$v_T(s_T,e^{T-1}) = ps_T(e^{T-1},0) + qs_T(e^{T-1},1) \quad (49a)$$

and

$$v_T(1,e^{T-1}) \quad = \quad p + q \tag{49b}$$

for some real numbers p and q. From the structure of the price process we, then, use

$$v_T(s_T,e^{T-1}) \;=\; s_{T-1}(e^{T-1}) \;=\; pus_{T-1}(e^{T-1}) \;+\; qds_{T-1}(e^{T-1})$$

So we have to solve

$$1 = pu + qd \qquad \text{and} \qquad b_{T-1} = p + q$$

for real numbers p and q. The solution is

$$p = \frac{1 - db_{T-1}}{u-d} \qquad \text{and} \qquad q = \frac{ub_{T-1} - 1}{u-d}$$

which (naturally) coincides with our former result. Because the end-of-period wealth of the option does not expand the relevant return space (it is two-dimensional) the Corollary of Proposition 8 tells us that the option can be valued by means of v_T:

$$\begin{aligned} C_{T-1} &= v_T(f(s_T),e^{T-1}) \\ &= pf(us_{T-1}) + qf(ds_{T-1}) \end{aligned}$$

Then a procedure applies which is completely analogous to that used before. The following sections will show that (48) and (49a,b) are special cases of a quite general feature of arbitrage - free price systems.

4.4. THE STRUCTURE OF ASSET PRICES UNDER NO-ARBITRAGE CONDITIONS

4.4.1. The Statement of No-Arbitrage Conditions

In the following our aim is to verify that under quite general conditions the main structural properties of the two-state option pricing process carry over to a more general environment. The results to be obtained depend on the way by which profitable arbitrage will be excluded. We choose the following condition which relates arbitrage to free lunches (recall that we generally assume the conditions of Theorem 1 to hold, particularly: no spreads, effective arbitration, no transaction costs):

Standard free lunches are not possible. (A9)

By Proposition 7 we know that (A9) implies that the Law of One Price holds for every point in time (see the proof of the Corollary of Proposition 7). So all the results carry over which hold if the Law of One Price holds.

There are two related no-arbitrage conditions which have been used in the literature the first of which we already met when analysing the implications of the CAPM (Section 1.8.). Both, they refer to a one-period setting; we apply them to a one-period segment of the entire multi-period model; let e^t be a fixed history emerged up to t:

There is a number $R(e^t)$ such that $E(D_{t+1}(x,.) + c_{t+1}(x,.)|e^t) = R(e^t)c_t(x,e^t)$ holds for any portfolio which is riskless over (t,t+1] conditional on e^t. (10)

If x is a riskless portfolio over (t,t+1] and if $c_t(x,e^t) = 0$ holds, then $E(D_{t+1}(x,.) + c_{t+1}(x,.)|e^t) = 0$ must hold. (A11)

(A10) has been used by ROLL (1977) in a somewhat different form whereas (A11) is the no-arbitrage condition introduced by ROSS (1976, 1977) in developing his Arbitrage Pricing Theory. In a way (A10) states that all riskless portfolios must earn the same rate of return (which may well be equal -1!). (A11) states that a zero investment must not earn a sure return at all.

There are at least two more conditions suggested in the literature (HUBERMAN (1982), CHAMBERLAIN/ROTHSCHILD (1983)) which relate to limits in 'large' markets; they are designed to make the linear price functional continuous even in the limit of large markets. We will guarantee continuity without refering to such markets. It is worthwhile to mention that the number of assets may well be infinite within our model.

PROPOSITION 9: (A10) is equivalent to (A11).

PROOF: Suppose (A10) to hold and let x be a riskless portfolio which requires no investment; then by (A10) we find

$$E(D_{t+1}(x,.) + c_{t+1}(x,.)|e^t) = 0$$

which proves that (A10) implies (A11). We now show that the converse is true: given that (A11) holds pick up two riskless portfolios x and y such that (without loss of generality) $c_t(x,e^t)$ and $c_t(y,e^t)$ are non-zero. Then there is a real number $w \neq 0$ such that $c_t(x,e^t) = wc_t(y,e^t)$ and hence, $c_t(x-wy,e^t) = 0$ holds. By (A11) we conclude:

$$E(D_{t+1}(x,.) + c_{t+1}(x,.)|e^t) = wE(D_{t+1}(y,.) + c_{t+1}(y,.)|e^t)$$

and, hence,

$$\frac{E(D_{t+1}(x,.) + c_{t+1}(x,.)|e^t)}{c_t(x,e^t)} = \frac{E(D_{t+1}(y,.) + c_{t+1}(y,.)|e^t)}{c_t(y,e^t)}$$

which completes our proof.

In (A10) it is possible that $R(e^t)$ becomes zero. This is the case when all riskless portfolios have zero return. Then it may well be that, in spite, the required investment is non-zero. This is an obvious shortcoming of (A10) and (A11). We therefore strengthen (A10) to:

(A10) is true together with $R(e^t)$ being non-zero. (A12)

We can now show that (A12) implies a kind of a one-period version of the Law of One Price which, in general, is weaker then the multiperiod version which we use:

ONE-PERIOD LAW OF ONE PRICE: The *one-period Law of One Price* is said to hold (at t and conditional on e^t) if

$$D_{t+1}(x,e^t,..) + c_{t+1}(x,e^t,..) = D_{t+1}(y,e^t,..) + c_{t+1}(y,e^t,..) \qquad (50)$$

almost surely, conditional on e^t implies $c_t(x,e^t) = c_t(y,e^t)$.

REMARKS: (i) Obviously, the one-period Law of One Price is the LOP as used in Section 1.8.

(ii) The Law of One Price in its multi-period form clearly implies the one-period Law of One Price.

PROPOSITION 10: (A12) implies the one-period of One Price.

PROOF: Assume (50) to hold. Then x-y is a riskless portfolio over $(t,t+1]$. (50) and (A10) together imply $R(e^t)c_t(x-y,e^t) = 0$ and by $R(e^t) \neq 0$ we get $c_t(x,e^t) = c_t(y,e^t)$, our assertion.

Interestingly, the one-period Law of One Price reveals a shortcoming which is symmetric to that of (A10) and prevents a proof of equivalence to (A12): it may well be the case that a riskless portfolio with a non-zero return does not require any investment. This does not provide a free lunch today, but a free lunch tomorrow. This is excluded by (A12). But there is still a shortcoming with (A12): if $R(e^t)$ turns out to be negative we have the unpleasant case that a *positive* riskless return requires a *negative* investment which makes possible two free lunches, simultaneously: today ***and*** tomorrow. We therefore strengten (A10) even further:

There is a positive number $R(e^t)$ such that $E(D_{t+1}(x,.) +$ (A13)
$+ c_{t+1}(x,.)|e^t) = R(e^t)c_t(x,e^t)$ for any portfolio x which is riskless over $(t,t+1]$.

We now show that there is a close relationship between (A9) and (A13):

PROPOSITION 11: (A9) implies that (A13) holds for $t = 0,\dots,T-1$ and almost all e^t.

PROOF: We first show that (A9) implies (A11). Assume e^t and a riskless portfolio x be given with $c_t(x,e^t) = 0$ and

$$E(D_{t+1}(x,.) + c_{t+1}(x,.)|e^t) > 0$$

Then a free lunch is possible by purchasing x at t conditional on e^t and liquidating it at t+1, also conditional on e^t. Hence, by (A9) $E(D_{t+1}(x,.) + c_{t+1}(x,.)|e^t)$ must be zero which implies (A11), which in turn implies (A10) by Proposition 9. It remains to show that $R(e^t)$ is positive. Suppose $R(e^t) \leq 0$; without loss of generality let $c_t(x,e^t)$ be non-negative (otherwise -x will do). Now sell x at t conditional on e^t and liquidate one period later. By (A10) and $R(e^t) \leq 0$ this provides for a free lunch at t and/or t+1. This completes our proof.

It is easily seen that the converse of Proposition 11 is not true: consider the one-period case with a safe asset with return zero and one other asset with a non-negative return which is positive with non-zero probability. If the prices for both assets would be zero this would not contradict (A13) but (A9): the second asset would provide a free lunch tomorrow. Thus it seems reasonable to start from (A9) as our basic no-arbitrage condition. We should well have in mind that (A9) implies the Law of One Price as well as (A13).

4.4.2. The Implications of "No Free Lunches" for the Two-State Option Pricing

In order to give some insight into the additional structure which is imposed by assuming no free lunches to be possible beyond the Law of One Price, we will investigate what we can deduce from (A9) in the case of two-state option pricing.

We assume the stock price s_0 and the jump variables u and d to be positive with d strictly smaller than u. We now show that p and q as given above must be positive and that $d < 1/b_{T-1} < u$ must hold if (A9) is assumed. We first consider the sign of p and q: By assumption we know that s_{T-1} and s_T are positive. From (A9) we get $b_{T-1} > 0$ for, otherwise, there would be a standard free lunch possible. Now assume $1/b_{T-1} \leq d$; now sell s_{T-1}/b_{T-1} bonds and purchase one stock at T-1 conditional on e^{T-1}. The return in T is $s_T - (s_{T-1}/b_{T-1}) \geq s_T - s_{T-1}d$ which is positive with non-zero probability. But the investment in T-1 is $s_{T-1} - (s_{T-1}/b_{T-1})b_{T-1} = 0$ from which a free lunch is possible. Hence, $d < 1/b_{t-1}$ must hold. Now assume $u \leq 1/b_{T-1}$. In this case buy s_{T-1}/b_{T-1} bonds and sell a stock. The investment is zero, the return is given by $(s_{T-1}/b_{T-1}) - s_T \geq s_{T-1}u - s_T$ which is, again, positive with non-zero probability from which a free lunch is possible. In sum, $d < 1/b_{T-1} < u$ must hold. But then it is easily seen that p and q are positive.

return in every period up to t; of course, a coupon paying bond having no risk of default is sufficient. The same is true for the following basic valuation theorem which is the core of the Arbitrage Theory and which leads us back (in a sense) to the valuation formula (12) (and following) of the CAPM.

THEOREM 2: Under the conditions of Proposition 13 there is a non-negative random variable q_1 on $(E,\mathcal{E}_1,\mu)$ such that for every portfolio x we have:

$$c_0(x,e_0) = v_1(D_1(x,.) + c_1(x,.)) = \int_E q_1 \cdot (D_1(x,.) + c_1(x,.))\,d\mu \quad (49)$$

$$= E(q_1 \cdot (D_1(x,.) + c_1(x,.)))$$

PROOF: The proof is quite simple: because v_1 is a positive continuous linear functional on X_1 (Proposition 13) it can be extended to $\bar{v}_1$ on $Y_1 l_1$ under preservation of these properties by (R2) since X_1 contains in its positive cone an interior point of the positive cone of $Y_1 l_1$. By Riesz's Representation Theorem (cf. BACHMAN/NARICI (1966)) we know that q_1 exists which meets (49). By the fact that $\bar{v}_1$ is a positive functional it immediately follows that q_1 must be non-zero and non-negative. q_1 belongs to $\mathcal{L}_q$ where $p^{-1} + q^{-1} = 1$ holds.

Under the conditions of the Theorem we know that q_1 is non-negative and that

$$\int_E q_1 \, d\mu \neq 0$$

must hold. Therefore, R is well-defined by

$$R^{-1} = \int_E q_1 \, d\mu$$

It is now seen that by $d\mu^* = Rq_1 d\mu$ there is defined a probability measure μ^* on $(E,\mathcal{E}_1)$ in the following sense:

$$\mu^*(A) = R \int_A q_1 \, d\mu \quad \text{for all } A \in \mathcal{E}_1.$$

Naturally, μ^* is absolutely continuous with respect to μ, i.e.every event in $\mathcal{E}_1$ which has zero probability with respect to μ has zero probability with respect to μ^*. We summarize these results in the following corollary which is, in a somewhat special version, the martingale result as proved by HARRISON/KREPS (1979).

COROLLARY: Under the conditions of Theorem 2 the market value of any portfolio x can be written as the discounted expected value of its end-of-period wealth for a suitable probability measure μ^* which is absolutely continuous with respect to μ:

$$c_0(x,e_0) = \frac{1}{R} \int_E (D_1(x,.) + c_1(x,.))d\mu^* = \frac{1}{R} E_{\mu^*}(D_1(x,.) + c_1(x,.)) \qquad (50)$$

REMARK: R is in fact the gross rate of return of a riskless asset or portfolio if there exist any.

Theorem 2 and its Corollary generalize the results which we derived for the case of two-state option pricing to a general principle.

4.4.4. The Multiperiod Case

The results just derived for the one-period case easily extend to several periods by iteration. We only sketch out the procedure assuming that there are no pay-outs. The one-period result applies to yield:

$$c_0(x,e_0) = \int_E q_0^t \cdot c_t(x,.)\,d\mu = E(q_0^t c_t(x,.))$$

for a suitable non-negative random variable q_0^t. In the same way we get, conditional on e^t:

$$c_t(x,e^t) = \int_E q_t^T \cdot c_T(x,.)\,d\mu(e^t,.) = E(q_t^T c_T(x,.)|e^t)$$

for some suitable non-negative q_t^T and the transition probability $\mu(e^t,.)$ which operates on $(E_{t+1},\mathcal{E}_{t+1})$. Combining these results achieves

$$c_0(x,e_0) = \int_E q_0^t E(q_t^T c_T(x,.)|e^t)\,d\mu = E(q_0^t q_t^T c_T(x,.))$$

By iteration we get:

$$c_o(x,e_o) = E(q_1 \cdot q_2 \cdot \ldots \cdot q_t \cdot c_t(x,.)) \quad \text{for all } t = 1,\ldots,T \tag{51}$$

and for suitable non-negative random variables q_h (h=1,...,T) which are defined on $(E,\mathcal{E}^h)$. These variables can be interpreted as stochastic discount factors each applying to a particular period of time.

It is now an easy task to derive the special equation (48) related to two-state option pricing from the general principle (51): From Section 4.3.2. we know that

$$q_h = \begin{cases} p/w_u & \text{for the "jump up" case} \\ q/w_d & \text{for the "jump down" case} \end{cases}$$

must hold when w_u (w_d, respectively) is the transition probability of up (down, respectively). By forming the expectation (51) these probabilities clearly drop out so that (48) obtains.

5. THE STRUCTURE OF ASSET RETURNS AND MEAN VARIANCE EFFICIENCY UNDER NO-ARBITRAGE CONDITIONS

In this section which is the last devoted to the development of the theory, we confine ourselves to the one-period case in the sense that only relations between end-of-period wealth positions and their initial market values are concerned; the period in question is arbitrarily depicted from the whole history, so we do not analyse a one-period model but restrict ourselves to the consideration of just one period in time. We assume the conditions of Theorem 2 to hold and, additionally, we assume the variances of the end-of-period wealth positions to be finite; in fact, we consider L(x) as elements of $\mathcal{L}_2(E,\mathcal{E}_1,\mu) = Y_1$. The return space is denoted by X and is, therefore, a subspace of the Hilbert space Y_1 (in the following we suppress the subscripts where there is no danger of confusion). In this section we make use of the Hilbert space property of Y. We assume X to be closed in X in order to treat X as a Hilbert space by itself. If X is not closed we have to deal with its closure thereby being enforced to speak of limit end-of-period wealth positions (random variables which are arbitrarily close to being feasible end-of-period wealth positions). So all the results which will be derived will hold if X is not closed with the qualification that "end-of-period wealth" is to be understood as "limit end-of-period wealth". In this way CHAMBERLAIN/ROTHSCHILD (1983) treat similar problems as we do; the results given below are partly in the same spirit but will be derived quite differently.

5.1. THE STRUCTURE OF ASSET RETURNS

The assumptions just made imply that asset prices and market values of portfolios can be written as a positive and continuous linear functional on a Hilbert space X. Such functionals allow for a special representation by Riesz's Representation Theorem for Hilbert spaces: there is a uniquely determined q which belongs to X (i.e. is a feasible end-of-period wealth position) such that

$$c_0(x) \quad = \quad E(qL(x))$$

holds for every portfolio; in the following we suppress the dependence of c_0 on e_0. It is important to note that q is uniquely determined and that there is a portfolio x_q such that $q = L(x_q)$ holds; so we have $c_o(x_q) = E(qL(x_q)) = E(q^2)$.

Since the expectation operator is a positive and continuous linear functional, too, we have, in consequence, a uniquely determined random variable e which belongs to X such that for every portfolio x we get

$$E(L(x)) = E(eL(x)) .$$

Of course, e = 1 must hold if and only if there is a riskless portfolio or asset. As well as q, e can be interpreted as the end-of-period wealth position of some portfolio x_e; so we have $c_o(x_e) = E(eq) = E(q)$. From $E(e^2) = E(e)$ we see by $E(e^2) = E(e)^2 + var(e)$ and, hence, $E(e) = E(e)^2 + var(e)$ which implies $E(e) \geq E(e)^2$ and, thus, $E(e) \leq 1$; additionally, $E(e) = 1$ holds if and only if there is a riskless portfolio or asset.

We now can state the main result concerning the structure of asset returns:

PROPOSITION 14: Suppose $E(q^2) - E(q)^2/E(e) \neq 0$; then to any end-of-period wealth $w \in X$ which can be achieved by some portfolio there is a unique representation of the form:

$$w = a_w e - \beta_w(q - \frac{c_o(x_e)}{E(e)} e) + h_w \tag{52}$$

where a_w and β_w are real numbers and $E(h_w) = E(q - \frac{c_o(x_e)}{E(e)} e) =$

$$= cov(e,h_w) = cov(q,h_w) = cov(q - \frac{c_o(x_e)}{E(e)} e, e) = 0 \text{ holds.}$$

REMARK: In the following we will use the abbreviation

$$\hat{q} = -\{ q - \frac{c_o(x_e)}{E(e)} e \} .$$

If there is a riskless asset then $\hat{q} = E(q) - q$ holds. The assumption in Proposition 14 concerning q now reads: $var(\hat{q}) \neq 0$. In harmony with the usage within the CAPM framework we call $\hat{q}$ the *scarcity indicator* of the price system.

PROOF: First observe that $E(e) = E(e^2) \neq 0$ must hold for, otherwise, every portfolio would have zero expectation, but we assumed the positive cone of X to have a non-empty interior. Now define N(f) to be the null space to any linear functional f; N(E) is then the space of end-of-period wealth positions with zero expectation. Since we know that e does not belong to N(E) we can decompose X as the following direct sum:

$$X = [e] \oplus N(E) .$$

Now observe

$$E(\hat{q}) = -\left\{E(q) - \frac{c_0(x_e)}{E(e)} E(e)\right\} = -\left\{E(q) - c_0(x_e)\right\} = 0 .$$

Hence, $\hat{q}$ belongs to N(E). We define the following linear functional g by $g(.) = \mathrm{cov}(.,\hat{q})$. The intersection of N(g) and N(E) is a subspace of N(E). Now

$$\mathrm{var}(\hat{q}) = g(\hat{q}) =$$

$$= E(q^2) - 2\frac{c_0(x_e)}{E(e)} E(qe) + \frac{c_0(x_e)^2}{E(e)^2} E(e^2) =$$

$= E(q^2) - \frac{E(q)^2}{E(e)}$ holds which is non-zero by assumption. Our assertion now easily follows from the direct sum decomposition

$$N(E) = [\hat{q}] \oplus (N(g) \cap N(E))$$

which completes our proof.

Remark that (52) conveys an analogy to the CAPM: the first part of the r.h.s. refers to the expectation, the second term to the current price system; e plays the role of a zero-beta portfolio. In addition we see that the term h_w does not have any risk influence on the market value of w:

$$v_1(w) = E(qw) = a_w E(q) + \beta_w E(q\hat{q}) + E(qh_w)$$

where $E(q\hat{q}) = -\mathrm{var}(\hat{q}) \neq 0$ by assumption. But $E(qh_w) = \mathrm{cov}(q,h_w) =$

$= \mathrm{cov}(q,h_w) - \frac{c_0(x_e)}{E(e)} \mathrm{cov}(e,h_w) = -\mathrm{cov}(\hat{q},h_w) = 0$ holds which proves our assertition. In consequence it seems reasonable to speak of h_w as the *unsystematic* component and of e and $\hat{q}$ as the *systematic* component of asset returns.

It is easily verified that

$$a_w = \frac{E(w)}{E(e)} \quad \text{and} \quad \beta_w = \frac{\text{cov}(w,\hat{q})}{\text{var}(\hat{q})}$$

hold. We therefore have for the market value of any end-of-period wealth w:

$$v_1(w) = \frac{c_o(x_e)}{E(e)} E(w) - \text{cov}(w,\hat{q}) \qquad (53)$$

which has an appealing similarity to the CAPM valuation formula. It remains to analyse the case when $\text{var}(\hat{q})$ vanishes. The answer is given by the next proposition:

PROPOSITION 15: If $\text{var}(\hat{q}) = 0$ holds, risk neutral pricing obtains.

PROOF: A look on the proof of Proposition 14 makes clear that the decomposition $X = [e] \circ N(E)$ still remains valid. Let be $w = a_w e + \hat{h}_w$ with $E(\hat{h}_w) = 0$. Then

$$v_1(w) = E(qw) = a_w E(q) + E(q\hat{h}_w)$$

holds. Now

$$E(q\hat{h}_w) = \text{cov}(h_w,q) =$$

$$= \text{cov}(\hat{h}_w,q) - \frac{c_o(x_e)}{E(e)} \cdot \text{cov}(\hat{h}_w,e) = -\text{cov}(\hat{h}_w,\hat{q}) = 0$$

because $\text{var}(\hat{q}) = 0$.This completes the proof.

Proposition 14 and 15 imply that (53) holds in either case. The term $c_o(x_e)/E(e)$ is the reciprocal of the expected gross rate of return on the end-of-period wealth position e, i.e. the expected gross rate of return to zero-beta portfolios. We formally write R^{-1} for this term. If R^{-1} is non-zero, as it is if there is a riskless asset or portfolio, (53) can be written in the following way in terms of rates of return (by R_q and R_w, respectively, we denote the gross rates of return to q and w, respectively):

$$E(R_w) - R = \frac{E(R_q) - R}{cov(R_q, R_q-(E(R_q)/E(e))e)} cov(R_w, R_q-(E(R_q)/E(e))e) \quad (54a)$$

which, if there exists a riskless portfolio or asset, simply reduces to:

$$E(R_w) - R = \frac{E(R_q) - R}{var(R_q)} cov(R_w, R_q) \quad (54b)$$

(54a) and (54b) are the analoga to the classical CAPM formula in terms of rates of return as given by (11c).

5.2. MEAN-VARIANCE EFFICIENCY

We come now to our last results in the development of Arbitrage Theory: to connections between mean-variance efficiency and no-arbitrage conditions. The first result is contained in Proposition 16:

PROPOSITION 16: Suppose that pricing is not risk-neutral. Then any mean-variance efficient end-of-period wealth $\hat{w}$ has the following three properties (note that $\hat{w}$ has, like every end-of-period wealth position, a representation

$$\hat{w} = \frac{E(\hat{w})}{E(e)} e + ßq̂ + h)$$

(i) $\hat{w}$ has no unsystematic component, i.e. $h = 0$.

(ii) ß is strictly positive.

(iii) $v_1(\hat{w}) \geq 0$ implies $E(\hat{w}) \geq 0$.

PROOF: From the above-mentioned representation of $\hat{w}$ we get

$$v_1(\hat{w}) = R^{-1}(E(\hat{w}) + ßE(q\hat{q})$$

Now take $r > 0$ and define an end-of-period wealth

$$w = \frac{E(\hat{w})}{E(e)} e + (ß + r)\hat{q}$$

We now show that w will dominate $\hat{w}$ if (i) or (ii) was not true. First we note that $w = \hat{w} + r\hat{q}$ and, therefore, $E(w) = E(\hat{w})$ and $v_1(w) = v_1(\hat{w}) + rv(\hat{q})$ and, hence, $v_1(w) < v_1(\hat{w})$ because of $r > 0$ and

$v_1(\hat{q}) = E(q\hat{q}) = -\mathrm{var}(\hat{q}) < 0$. Now suppose h non-zero. Compute the variances of w and $\hat{w}$, respectively:

$$\mathrm{var}(w) = \frac{E(\hat{w})^2}{E(e)^2}\mathrm{var}(e) + (\beta + r)^2 \mathrm{var}(\hat{q})$$

$$\mathrm{var}(\hat{w}) = \frac{E(\hat{w})^2}{E(e)^2}\mathrm{var}(e) + \beta^2 \mathrm{var}(\hat{q}) + \mathrm{var}(h)$$

Now look at the difference $\mathrm{var}(w) - \mathrm{var}(\hat{w}) = ((\beta+r)^2 - \beta^2)\mathrm{var}(\hat{q}) -$ $- \mathrm{var}(h)$. By a suitable reduction of r we can make the bracketed term arbitrarily close to zero such that the whole difference must be negative as long as var(h) is non-zero. In that case w would strictly dominate $\hat{w}$ which is impossible since $\hat{w}$ is mean-variance efficient; this proves (i). Additionally, since var(h) must be zero, the difference will only be positive if β is positive which proves (ii). In order to prove (iii) assume $E(\hat{w}) < 0$ and $v_1(\hat{w}) \geq 0$ for some efficient $\hat{w}$. But then $E(-\hat{w}) > 0 > E(\hat{w}), v_1(-\hat{w}) \leq 0 \leq v_1(\hat{w})$ and $\mathrm{var}(-\hat{w}) = \mathrm{var}(\hat{w})$ must hold, i.e. $-\hat{w}$ would strictly dominate $\hat{w}$ which is impossible.

The converse to Proposition 16 is true under slightly more restrictive conditions:

PROPOSITION 17: Suppose that pricing is not risk-neutral. If $\hat{w}$ meets (i) and (ii), and if $E(q) \geq 0$ holds then $\hat{w}$ meets (iii). If in addition, $E(\hat{w}) \geq 0$ holds then $\hat{w}$ is mean-variance efficient.

REMARK: The condition $E(q) = v_1(1) > 0$ is met if there is a riskless asset or portfolio.

PROOF: First observe that $v_1(\hat{q}) = E(q\hat{q}) = -\mathrm{var}(\hat{q}) < 0$ since no risk-neutral pricing obtains. Our first assertion (iii) is a simple consequence of (i), (ii) and $E(q) \geq 0$. Now assume

$$\hat{w} = \frac{E(\hat{w})}{E(e)} e + \beta\hat{q}$$

be given which meets (i) and (ii). Assume an end-of-period wealth

$$w = \frac{E(w)}{E(e)} e + \beta_w \hat{q} + h_w$$

which dominates $\hat{w}$, i.e. $E(w) \geq E(\hat{w})$, $v_1(w) \leq v_1(\hat{w})$ and $var(w) \leq var(\hat{w})$.

$$v_1(w) = E(w)\frac{E(q)}{E(e)} + \beta_w E(q\hat{q})$$

$$v_1(\hat{w}) = E(\hat{w})\frac{E(q)}{E(e)} + \beta E(q\hat{q})$$

From $v_1(w) \leq v_1(\hat{w})$ we find $(E(\hat{w}) - E(w))\frac{E(q)}{E(e)} + (\beta-\beta_w)E(q\hat{q}) \geq 0$

and, hence, $(\beta-\beta_w)E(q\hat{q}) \geq (E(w) - E(\hat{w}))\frac{E(q)}{E(e)} \geq 0$ and, consequently,

$\beta \leq \beta_w$. From (ii) we know that β is strictly positive and, therefore, $\beta^2 \leq \beta_w^2$ must hold. We can now calculate the respective variances of w and $\hat{w}$; we find

$$var(w) = \frac{E(w)^2}{E(e)^2}var(e) + \beta_w^2\, var(\hat{q}) + var(h_w)$$

$$var(\hat{w}) = \frac{E(\hat{w})^2}{E(e)^2}var(e) + \beta^2 var(\hat{q})$$

Since $E(\hat{w}) \geq 0$ holds we can conclude that $var(w) > var(\hat{w})$ as long as $var(h_w) \neq 0$. But then $var(w) = var(\hat{w})$ and, thus, $h_w = 0$, $E(w) = E(\hat{w})$ and $\beta = \beta_w$ and, therefore, $w = \hat{w}$ which completes our proof.

Proposition 16 and 17 make very clear that the statement on systematic and unsystematic parts of asset returns as made by the CAPM simply is a consequence of no-arbitrage conditions. It is thereby shown that much of the capital market theory, particularly, the central role of mean variance efficiency, stems from formal correspondances to no-arbitrage conditions rather than from individual preferences: it is seen that the "pricing portfolio" $\hat{q}$ can be substituted by any arbitrary mean-variance efficient end-of-period wealth as is made clear by Proposition 16. Proposition 17 gives sufficient conditions under which there exist such efficient portfolios.

As a simple nice corollary one can calculate the set of mean-variance efficient combinations of expected rates of return and their corresponding standard deviations to arrive at the well-known *capital market line*:

COROLLARY: Let μ(σ, respectively) be the expected rate of return (the standard deviation of the rate of return, respectively) of end-of-period wealth positions. The set of mean-variance efficient combinations fulfills the following equation:

$$\sigma^2 = \frac{var(e)}{E(e)^2}\mu^2 + var(R_{\hat{q}})\left(\frac{\mu - R}{R}\right)^2 \qquad (55)$$

where R is the expected gross rate of return to zero-beta portfolios and $R_{\hat{q}}$ is the gross rate of return to $\hat{q}$. If there is a riskless asset or portfolio then R is its gross rate of return and (55) collapses to

$$\sigma = var(R_{\hat{q}}) \frac{\mu - R}{R} \qquad (56)$$

the capital market line.

The proof is left to the reader.

The circle has been closed: we started with mean-variance efficiency as a concept of individual preferences and saw that it implies a kind of a Law of One Price. We then analysed financial asset markets which do not allow for risk-free arbitrage profits and came to the conclusion that mean-variance efficiency is closely related to those markets, although nothing has been said about individual preferences. It is only the mathematical qualification of the variance operator to reflect, in a successful way, the uncertainty of asset returns. As has been argued in a preceding section, if there are arbitrage opportunities there is no need for individual investors to properly outweigh the uncertainty and the level of portfolio returns. But if arbitrage opportunities are excluded the individual investor faces a certain rate of substitution between risk and the level of its end-of-period wealth positions. This fact is reflected by (55) and/or by (56). This nevertheless does not at all mean that individual investors (should) pick their portfolios from (55) or (56) - this fact has already been observed when non-marketable assets has been introduced into the CAPM - . It only means that in the absence of risk-free arbitrage opportunities there necessarily is a trade-off between "*risk and returns*" which can effectively be measured in terms of mathematical expectation and variance of asset returns. So ROLL's statement is easy to follow that the empirical essence of the CAPM is that the 'dummy variable'

$\hat{q}$, the *scarcity indicator*, which is empirically undetermined whithin our theory of arbitrage-free asset markets, must be the return of the market portfolio within the CAPM, i.e. the empirical essence is that the market portfolio is mean-variance efficient (ROLL (1977)) since by Proposition 16 we know that all efficient portfolios are positively correlated linear transformations of each other and of the scarcity indicator as well. Hence, the return to the market portfolio can play the role of $\hat{q}$ if and only if the market portfolio is mean-variance efficient.

6. SOME SELECTED APPLICATIONS

6.1. OPTIONS

6.1.1. No Early Exercise of an American Call (MERTON (1973 b))

Let s_t be the price of the underlying stock at point in time t; T be the expiration date and B the exercise price of the American Call; C_t be the option price at t. We assume that the stock does not pay dividends before the option expires. Let be A_t the event when the call is exercised at point in time t (clearly A_t belongs to $\mathcal{E}^t$). Of course,

$$s_t(e^t) - B \geq C_t(e^t)$$

must hold for all $e^t \in A_t$ for, otherwise, it would be better to sell the option than to exercise from which a free lunch would be possible. The supposed exercise strategy leads to the following consumption pattern over time:

$$u_t(e^t) = \begin{cases} s_t(e^t) - B & \text{for } e^t \in A_t \\ 0 & \text{otherwise} \end{cases} \qquad (t=1,\ldots,T-1)$$

and

$$u_T(e^T) = \begin{cases} \max(s_T(e^T) - B, 0) & \text{for } e^T \notin \bigcup_{t=1}^{T-1} A_t \\ 0 & \text{otherwise} \end{cases}$$

We now construct an alternative consumption pattern: if $e^t \in A_t$ happens sell short one stock and invest amount B risklessly over the rest of the expiration period. The resulting consumption pattern will be

$$\hat{u}_t(e^t) = \begin{cases} s_t(e^t) - B & \text{for } e^t \in A_t \\ 0 & \text{otherwise} \end{cases} \qquad (t=1,\ldots,T-1)$$

$$\hat{u}_T(e^T) = \max(s_T(e^T) - B,0) + \begin{cases} 0 & \text{for } e^T \notin \bigcup_{t=1}^{T-1} A_t \\ BR_t^T(e^t) - s_T(e^T) & \text{for } e^T \in A_t \end{cases}$$

where $R_t^T(e^t)$ is the gross rate of return of a riskless investment over period (t,T) conditional on the event $e^t \in A_t$. Now look at some event e^t in A_t when the option has been exercised in the first strategy. For the second strategy we get at the expiration date conditional on this event:

$$\hat{u}_T = \max(s_T - B,0) + BR_t^T(e^t) - s_T$$

$$= \max(B(R_t^T(e^t) - 1), BR_t^T(e^t) - s_T) > 0$$

as long as the riskless rate of return is greater than zero. Thus, we have constructed a situation where a free lunch is possible provided that riskless assets earn a positive rate of return: The exercise strategy u is dominated by strategy $\hat{u}$.

6.1.2. Put-Call-Parity (STOLL (1969))

Suppose a European Put and a European Call be given having the same exercise price B and the same expiration date T both written on the same non dividend paying stock s_t. The European Call is characterized by

$$\max(s_T - B,0)$$

while the European Put earns

$$\max(B - s_T,0) .$$

Now observe

$$\max(s_T - B,o) - \max(B - s_T,0) =$$

$$\max(s_T - B,0) + \min(s_T - B,0) = s_T - B.$$

Applying the price functional v^T yields:

$$v^T(\max(s_T - B,0)) - v^T(\max(B - s_T,0)) = v^T(s_T) - v^T(B) .$$

If C_0 is the current price of the European Call and P_0 the current price of the European Put we get the *Put-Call-Parity*:

$$C_0 + \frac{B}{R_0^T} = P_0 + s_0 \qquad (57)$$

6.1.3. The Valuation of Contingent Claims in Discrete Time (RUBINSTEIN (1976), BRENNAN (1979))

Contingent claims can successfully be valued in discrete time when distributional assumptions are imposed on the model of arbitrage-free financial markets. The assumptions concern the joint probability distribution of the underlying security and the *scarcity indicator* $\hat{q}$ whose existence is guaranteed in arbitrage-free financial asset markets. There are several combinations which work; we choose one of them which produces a consistent model of asset prices over time (cf. WILHELM (1984)).

Let S be the price of the underlying security at the relevant point in time and $Q = \log q$ be the logarithm of $q = 1/(1+r) - \hat{q}$ where r is the riskless rate of interest. We assume S and Q to follow a joint normal distribution (the classical BLACK/SCHOLES - formula would obtain if Q and log S follow a joint normal distribution). The contingent claim be described by the function g(S). The market value of the contingent claim is, therefore, be given by

$$v_1(g(S)) = E(q \cdot g(S)) = E(g(S)e^Q) .$$

Obviously,

$$E(g(S)e^Q) = E(g(S)E(e^Q|S))$$

must hold. Standard knowledge on normally distributed variables tells

$$E(e^Q|S) = \exp\{E(Q|S) + \tfrac{1}{2}\operatorname{var}(Q|S)\}$$

On the other hand we know (FELLER (1971, p. 86)):

$$E(Q|S) = E(Q) + \frac{cov(Q,S)}{var(S)}(S - E(S))$$

and

$$var(Q|S) = var(Q) - \frac{cov(Q,S)^2}{var(S)}$$

So we have

$$E(e^Q|S) = \exp\{ E(Q) + \frac{1}{2}var(Q) + \frac{cov(Q,S)}{var(S)}(S - E(S)) - \frac{1}{2}\frac{cov(Q,S)^2}{var(S)} \}$$

$$= R^{-1} \exp\{ \frac{cov(Q,S)}{var(S)}(S - E(S)) - \frac{1}{2} \frac{cov(Q,S)^2}{var(S)} \}$$

because of

$$\exp\{ E(Q) + \frac{1}{2} var(Q) \} = E(e^Q) = E(q) = 1/(1+r) = R^{-1}$$

We now see

$$v_1(g(S)) = \frac{1}{\sqrt{2\pi}} \frac{R^{-1}}{\sqrt{var(S)}} \int_{-\infty}^{+\infty} g(x) \exp\{\frac{cov(Q,S)}{var(S)}(x-E(S)) - \frac{1}{2} \frac{cov(Q,S)^2}{var(S)} \} \cdot$$

$$\cdot \exp\{ - \frac{1}{2} \frac{(x-E(S))^2}{var(S)} \} dx$$

If we use, as usual, N(.) for the standardized normal distribution function we get:

$$v_1(g(S)) = \frac{R^{-1}}{\sqrt{var(S)}} \int_{-\infty}^{+\infty} g(x) N'(\frac{x - E(S) - cov(Q,S)}{var(S)}) dx \qquad (58)$$

Observe that (58) exhibits a risk neutral valuation if we use as probability the normal distribution for the stock price with variance var(S) and expectation E(S) + cov(Q,S). This is in accordance with the martingale result as stated in Corollary of Theorem 2. By a transformation of variables we get

$$v_1(g(S)) = R^{-1} \int_{-\infty}^{+\infty} g(z\sqrt{var(S)} + E(S) + cov(Q,S)) \, dN(z)$$

We are now interested in the term cov(Q,S). By an argument proved by RUBINSTEIN (1976) we know

$$\mathrm{cov}(q,S) = \mathrm{cov}(e^Q,S) = E(e^Q)\,\mathrm{cov}(Q,S)$$

Thus, cov(Q,S) = R cov(q,S) holds. But

$$S_0 = E(qS) = E(q)E(S) + \mathrm{cov}(Q,S) = R^{-1}E(S) + \mathrm{cov}(q,S)$$

which implies $R\mathrm{cov}(q,S) = RS_0 - E(S)$.
So we finally get

$$v_1(g(S)) = R^{-1} \int_{-\infty}^{+\infty} g(z\sqrt{var(S)} + RS_0)\, dN(z) \qquad (59)$$

which is an analogon to the BLACK/SCHOLES-formula of option pricing: the value of the contingent claim only depends on the current value and the variance of the underlying security and on the riskless rate of return. For an extension to the case of several underlying securities we refer to WILHELM (1984).

It is an easy task to specify (59) for an American Call by

$$g(S) = \max\{S-B, 0\}$$

where B is the exercise price of the option. (62) then reads with $\sigma(S) = \sqrt{var(S)}$

$$v_1(g(S)) = \sigma(S) \int_{\frac{B-RS_0}{\sigma(S)}} z\,dN(z) + (RS_0-B)(1 - N(\frac{B-RS_0}{\sigma(S)})) \qquad (60)$$

Since N" = - zN' holds we get

$$v_1(g(S)) = (RS_0-B)(1 - N(\frac{B-RS_0}{\sigma(S)})) + \sigma(S)N'(\frac{B-RS_0}{\sigma(S)}) \qquad (61)$$

which is an alternative option pricing formula. If the exercise price equals the theoretically predicted forward price RS_0 of the stock we get the price of an *even premium contract* (as marketed in Zurich or Paris) simply by:

$$v_1(g(S)) = \frac{\sigma(S)}{\sqrt{2\pi}} \quad . \tag{62}$$

6.2. FORWARD AND FUTURES CONTRACTS

6.2.1. Interest Rate Parity Theory of Foreign Exchange Rates (KEYNES (1923))

Let the rate of interest for riskless assets over one period of time be i_h for the domestic country and i_f for the foreign country. The exchange rate be x_o, the forward rate x_1. In terms of the domestic currency it is a riskless operation to purchase $1/x_o$ units of the foreign currency, to invest this amount into a riskless asset to arrive at $(1+i_f)/x_o$ and to sell forward this amount, simultaneously, over one period of time which results in $x_1(1+i_f)/x_o$ units in the domestic currency. Hence we have an end-of-period wealth of $x_1(1+i_f)/x_o$ which has a market price $v_1((1+i_f)x_1/x_o) = 1$ which had to be paid for the foreign currency money. If the market is arbitrage-free a riskless end-of-period wealth of one unit must be priced at $v_1(1) = 1/(1+i_h)$ and, therefore

$$v_1((1+i_f)x_1/x_o) = x_1(1+i_f)/(x_o(1+i_h))$$

The Law of One Price requires

$$\frac{x_1}{x_o}\,\frac{1+i_f}{1+i_h} = 1$$

From this we get

$$\frac{x_1}{x_o} = \frac{1+i_h}{1+i_f} = 1 + \frac{i_h - i_f}{1+i_f}$$

or

$$\frac{x_1}{x_o} - 1 = \frac{i_h - i_f}{1+i_f}$$

and, finally,

$$\frac{x_1 - x_o}{x_o} = \frac{i_h - i_f}{1 + i_f} \tag{63}$$

The left-hand side of (63) is the so-called *swap rate*. Interest Rate Parity Theory requires the *swap rate to equal* (approximately) *the interest rate differential*.

6.2.2. Forward and Futures Prices (COX/INGERSOLL/ROSS (1981))

a) *Forward Prices*

A forward contract is an agreement to buy (to sell) a specified amount of a certain market object (commodity, currency, stock, bond, market index etc.) at a specified future date at a specified price, the forward price. We denote by p_t the price at t of the underlying market object, by $p_{t,T}$ the forward price at t for delivery at T and by $f_{t,T}$ the value of a living forward contract for delivery at T as observed at t. We assume that a storable good is underlying the contract with non-stochastic cash-flows h_t to be paid if one unit of the good is held over period (t-1,t); remark that these cash-flows can be storage costs, insurance costs etc. if positive, and can be coupon payments (on an underlying bond) if negative.

Since no money changes hands the current value $f_{o,T}$ for a contract agreed upon at t=0 must be zero, while on the other hand arbitrage-free markets require $f_{T,T} = p_T$. The consumption pattern associated with a forward contract is given by

$$u_t = 0 \qquad \text{for } t = 0,\ldots,T-1$$

$$u_T = p_{o,T} - p_T$$

The consumption pattern induced by the purchase at 0 and the sale at T of one unit of the commodity is given by

$$\hat{u}_o = -p_o$$

$$\hat{u}_t = -h_t \qquad \text{for } t = 1,\ldots,T-1$$

$$\hat{u}_T = p_T - h_T$$

In arbitrage-free markets we know

$$v^T((p_{o,T} - p_T)l_T) = \frac{p_{o,T}}{R_o^T} - v^T(p_T l_T) = 0$$

from the forward contract; from the second strategy we get:

$$p_o = - \sum_{t=1}^{T} v^T(h_t l_t) + v^T(p_T l_T) = - \sum_{t=1}^{T} \frac{h_t}{R_o^t} + v^T(p_T l_T)$$

Hence we see

$$v^T(p_T l_T) = p_o + \sum_{t=1}^{T} \frac{h_t}{R_o^t}$$

and, finally, we get

$$p_{o,T} - p_o = p_o(R_o^T - 1) + \sum_{t=1}^{T} \frac{R_o^T}{R_o^t} h_t \tag{64}$$

The left-hand side of (64) is called the *basis*. The right-hand side consists of the interest on the current market price and the (discounted) storage costs; this amount is sometimes called the *contango*. By the theoretical argument (64) the basis is predicted to equal the contango.

Consider finally the current value of a living forward contract:

$$f_{t,T} = v_t^T((p_{o,T} - p_T)l_T) = \frac{p_{o,T}}{R_t^T} - v_t^T(p_T l_T)$$

where

$$v_t^T(p_T l_T) = p_t + \sum_{r=t+1}^{T} \frac{h_r}{R_t^r}$$

must hold and, therefore,

$$f_{t,T} = \frac{p_{o,T}}{R_t^T} - p_t - \sum_{r=t+1}^{T} \frac{h_r}{R_t^r}$$

The consumption pattern associated with a *hedge* which will be liquidated at t is, thus, given as follows:

$$u_o = -p_o$$

$$u_r = -h_r \qquad \text{for } r = 1,\dots,t-1$$

$$u_t = -h_t + p_t + f_{t,T}$$

The interesting issue is the net payment at the liquidation date:

$$u_t = -h_t + p_t + p_{o,T}/R_t^T - p_t - \sum_{r=t+1}^{T} (h_r/R_t^r)$$

$$= p_{o,T}/R_t^T - h_t - \sum_{r=t+1}^{T} (h_r/R_t^r)$$

If the hedge for various possible reasons cannot be 'tailored' (this is only the case when liqudation is at T) there remains uncertainty to the extent that future interest rates are not known in advance at which the forward price will be discounted (not accounted for the storage costs).

b) *Futures Prices*

Futures contracts differ from forward contracts - aside from their higher degree of standardization - by their feature of daily settlement. The daily rise or fall of the futures price will be added to or substracted from, respectively, the customer's account whereas the contract will formally be renewed at the daily closing futures price. An expression for the futures price can be found by the following recursive procedure: look at the period T - 1, one period before delivery will take place; the characteristic is given by

$$u_T = p_{T-1,T} - p_T$$

because at T - 1 the contract will be renewed at the closing futures price $p_{T-1,T}$. As seen fromT-1, u_T has zero market value such that

$$v_{T-1}^T(p_{T-1,T} - p_T) = 0$$

as was the case for a forward contract. But because $p_{T-1,T}$ is non-stochastic from the perspective of T - 1 we get:

$$\frac{p_{T-1,T}}{R_{T-1}^{T}} = v_{T-1}^{T}(p_T)$$

and, thus,

$$p_{T-1,T} = v_{T-1}^{T}(R_{T-1}^{T} p_T)$$

Looking back to T - 2 yields

$$v_{T-2}^{T-1}(p_{T-2,T} - p_{T-1,T}) = 0$$

because at T - 1 the difference between the respective futures prices will be accounted for while the contract's value will be set to zero. Therefore we get:

$$\begin{aligned} p_{T-2,T} &= R_{T-2}^{T-1} v_{T-2}^{T-1}(R_{T-1}^{T} v_{T-1}^{T}(p_T)) \\ &= v_{T-2}^{T-1}(v_{T-1}^{T}(R_{T-2}^{T-1} \cdot R_{T-1}^{T} \cdot p_T)) \\ &= v_{T-2}^{T}(R_{T-2}^{T-1} \cdot R_{T-1}^{T} \cdot p_T) \end{aligned}$$

By induction one proves:

$$p_{o,T} = v^{T}(p_T \cdot \prod_{t=1}^{T} R_{t-1}^{t}) \qquad (65)$$

i.e. the futures price is the market value of a hypothetical market object which is given by the commodity price at the time of delivery, as if it was invested in short term bonds rolled over the intermediate periods. It is easily seen by comparing (64) and (65) that the futures price and the forward price coincide if the short term interest rates evolve non-stochastically over time which is highly unprobable.

6.3. CORPORATE FINANCIAL POLICY

6.3.1. The Valuation of Levered Firms (MODIGLIANI/MILLER (1958))

If the investment policy of a firm is given and if there are no taxes and no bankruptcy costs the future (uncertain) gross return X of a firm will be distributed to debt holders (X_D) and to equity holders

(X_E) such that $X = X_E + X_D$ according to some priority rule. If asset markets are arbitrage-free we have a linear price functional v_1 such that $v_1(X) = v_1(X_E+X_D) = v_1(X_E) + v_1(X_D)$ holds so that the value of the firm $v_1(X_E) + v_1(X_D)$ which is the sum of equity and debt in market values, is independent of the firm's capital structure (as long as v_1 is independent from the particular (X_E,X_D)-rule which is a difficult theoretical task).

6.3.2. The FISHER Separation Under Uncertainty (De ANGELO (1981))

Our next application concerns the investment decision under uncertainty. We assume each individual to search for *efficient* consumption patterns in a one-period framework . If C is the set of feasible consumption patterns (c_0,c_1) where c_1 is uncertain in general, then an efficient consumption pattern (c_0^*,c_1^*) requires

$$c_0^* = \max\{c_0 \mid (c_0,c_1) \in C \text{ and } c_1 = c_1^* \text{ almost certainly}\}$$

Now suppose the investor in question is endowed with a portfolio x_0 and has the opportunity to invest into a productive asset; the investment outlay is denoted by I, the return by g(I) which is uncertain. The set C of feasible consumption patterns is:

$$c_0 = P_0x_0 - P_0x_1 - I \geq 0 \qquad (66)$$

$$c_1 = Vx_1 + g(I) \qquad (67)$$

where V is the vector of returns of marketed assets and x_1 is the new portfolio of marketed assets. An efficient consumption pattern (c_0^*,c_1^*), thus, meets the following condition:

$$c_0^* = \max\{c_0 \mid c_0 = P_0(x_0-x_1) - I \geq 0 \text{ and } c_1^* = Vx_1 + g(I)\} \qquad (68)$$

We now assume that *the asset market is arbitrage-free* such that there is a linear price functional v.

From (68) we get

$$v(c_1^*) = v(V)x_1 + v(g(I)) = P_0x_1 + v(g(I))$$

and, hence,

$$P_0 x_1 = v(c_1^*) - v(g(I)) .$$

We now have to maximize

$$c_0 = P_0 x_0 - v(c_1^*) + v(g(I)) - I \qquad (69)$$

which will be maximized by the maximization of

$$v(g(I)) - I , \qquad (70)$$

the market value of the real investment opportunity, a preference-free objective function.

This would be the FISHER separation under uncertainty if there were not some severe problems:

(i) May v be applied to g(I) ?

(ii) Does the real project have an influence on the functional v ?

(iii) Does the real project have an influence on the initial prices P_0 ?

(iv) May (70) be maximized without individually determined constraints ?

A satisfactory answer to these questions cannot be given without additional assumptions. The assumptions are:

- *competitivity*: the real project has no influence on state dependent prices, i.e. no influence on the correct price functional v;
- *spanning*: for each investment volume I there is a portfolio y_I which duplicates g(I), i.e.

  $$g(I) = V \cdot y_I \text{ almost certainly}$$

- no *synergistic* or other *external* effects: V is independent of the real project.

We now see that problems (i) and (ii) disappear immediately. Since

$P_o = v(V)$ holds we solve problem (iii) by the competitivity assumption.

To solve problem (iv) assume x_1^* and I^* to solve problem (68) when $g(I^*) = V \cdot y_{I^*}$ holds, whereas I^{**} solves the unconstrained maximization problem (70). From spanning we know that there is a portfolio x_1^{**} such that

$$c_1^* = Vx_1^* + g(I^*) = Vx_1^{**} + g(I^{**}) \tag{71}$$

From the application of v to (71) we conclude

$$P_o x_1^* + v(g(I^*)) = P_o x_1^{**} + v(g(I^{**})) \tag{72}$$

From (66) we get

$$c_o^* = P_o x_o - P_o x_1^* - I^* \tag{73}$$

and

$$c_o^{**} = P_o x_o - P_o x_1^{**} - I^{**} \tag{74}$$

By assumption we know

$$v(g(I^*)) - I^* \leq v(g(I^{**})) - I^{**} \tag{75}$$

From (73) and (74) we conclude

$$c_o^{**} - c_o^* = P_o x_1^* - P_o x_1^{**} + I^* - I^{**} \tag{76}$$

From (72) we have

$$P_o x_1^* - P_o x_1^{**} = v(g(I^{**})) - v(g(I^*))$$

which, together with (76), yields:

$$c_o^{**} - c_o^* = v(g(I^{**})) - I^{**} - (v(g(I^*)) - I^*) \tag{77}$$

which is non-negative by (75) which proves our assertion. FISHER separation therefore holds under uncertainty if asset markets are arbitrage-free, if competitivity and spanning hold and if there are no synergistic or external effects of real investment projects.

6.4. ARBITRAGE THEORY AND ROSS's ARBITRAGE PRICING THEORY

In 'deriving' his Arbitrage Pricing Theory ROSS (1976,1977) starts from a factor structure of asset returns; let us denote by Δ the vector of mutually uncorrelated random factors with zero expectation which generate the returns of the marketed assets, these returns being denoted by the random vector V. With the matrix of *factor loadings* B we may write, therefore,

$$V = E(V) + B \cdot \Delta + \varepsilon \qquad (78)$$

where ε is the vector of residual random disturbances with zero expectation which superimpose the systematic influences of factors; $COV(\Delta,\varepsilon) = 0$ holds. Now consider a net portfolio change z which does not require additional funds nor produces additional income when it is executed, i.e.

$$P_0 \cdot z = 0 \qquad (79)$$

must hold. Such a portfolio change is called an *arbitrage portfolio*. The return of portfolio change z will be in the present context (it is now necessary to distinguish column and row vectors, respectively; generally, we treat vectors as column vectors, transposition is indicated by an apostrophe)

$$z'V = z'E(V) + z'B\Delta + z'\varepsilon \qquad (80)$$

Now, the no-arbitrage condition (A11) is assumed to hold: a riskless portfolio change z using no investment ((79)) must not have a nonzero expected return, i.e.

$$var(z'V) = 0 \text{ and } z'P_0 = 0 \text{ together imply } z'E(V) = 0 \qquad (81)$$

Using (80) in (81) we get that

$$z'B\,COV(\Delta,\Delta)B'z + z'COV(\varepsilon,\varepsilon)z = 0$$

implies

$$z'E(V) = 0$$

Without loss of generality COV(Δ,Δ) = I , I identity matrix, may be assumed. So, (81) now reads:

$$z'BB'z = 0 \text{ and } z'COV(\varepsilon,\varepsilon)z = 0 \text{ and } z'P_0 = 0 \quad (82)$$

together imply z'E(V) = 0

Clearly, z'BB'z = 0 implies z'B = 0 and, hence, (82) becomes:

$$z'B = 0 \text{ and } z'COV(\varepsilon,\varepsilon)z = 0 \text{ and } z'P_0 = 0 \quad (83)$$

together imply z'E(V) = 0

There is now an inaccurateness in the reasoning: it is (more or less explicitly) assumed (ROLL/ROSS (1980, p. 1078)) that z'B = 0 *always implies* z'COV(ε,ε)z by a kind of law of large numbers; this assumption is quite questionable. But in so doing, we arrive at:

$$z'B = 0 \text{ and } z'P_0 = 0 \text{ together imply } z'E(V) = 0 \quad (84)$$

By standard arguments in linear algebra it follows that P_0,E(V) and the columns of B must be linearly dependent, i.e.

$$P_0 = aE(V) + B \cdot \Lambda \quad (85)$$

must hold for a suitable real number a and an appropriate vector Λ . (85) is the central statement of the Arbitrage Pricing Theory; it means that asset prices can be explained by their expected values and the *systematic* risk components which measure the reagibility of asset returns with some few general factors:

$$B = COV(V,\Delta)$$

Λ is the vector of market prices per unit of systematic (covariance-) risk with respect to the factors Δ . Idiosyncratic risk (ε) seem to play no role in determining asset prices. This is the spirit of the arbitrage pricing theory; but as will be seen later by arbitrage theoretic arguments this is not necessarily the case.

In order to simplify our reasoning we assume a riskless portfolio with rate of return $r > -1$ to exist (for a narrower inspection of the general case see FRANKE (1984)); of course $a = \frac{1}{1+r}$ must hold. From Section 4.4.1. we know that with (81) there is a linear price functional v. Applying v to (78) we get:

$$P_0 = v(V) = \frac{1}{1+r}E(V) + B \cdot v(\Delta) + v(\varepsilon) \tag{86}$$

Suppose the number of factors be k and, without loss of generality, the upper (kxk)-submatrix B_0 of B be non-singular (otherwise rearrange factors accordingly); we write

$$B = \begin{pmatrix} B_0 \\ B_1 \end{pmatrix}; \quad P_0 = \begin{pmatrix} P_0^0 \\ P_0^1 \end{pmatrix}; \quad V = \begin{pmatrix} V^0 \\ V^1 \end{pmatrix}; \quad \varepsilon = \begin{pmatrix} \varepsilon^0 \\ \varepsilon^1 \end{pmatrix}$$

There is a certain matrix A such that

$$B_1 = A \cdot B_0$$

holds. Thus, we have

$$P_0^0 = \frac{1}{1+r}E(V^0) + B_0 v(\Delta) + v(\varepsilon^0) \tag{87}$$

and

$$P_0^1 = \frac{1}{1+r}E(V^1) + AB_0 v(\Delta) + v(\varepsilon^1) \tag{88}$$

We now show that the market prices Λ of systematic risk are, in part, determined by idiosyncratic risk influence. From Section 5.2. we know that there is a portfolio the return q of which obeys:

$$v(\Delta) = E(q \cdot \Delta) = COV(\Delta, q) \tag{89}$$

and

$$v(\varepsilon) = E(q \cdot \varepsilon) = COV(\varepsilon, q) \tag{90}$$

since $E(\Delta) = E(\varepsilon) = 0$ holds. Because q is a portfolio return there is a portfolio change $z_\star$ such that

$$q = z_\star' \cdot V = \frac{1}{1+r} z_\star' E(V) + z_\star' B \cdot \Delta + z_\star' \varepsilon \tag{91}$$

with $z_\star' E(V) = 1$. From (89) we conclude

$$v(\Delta) = z_*'B = b_q \tag{92}$$

and from (90) we see

$$v(\varepsilon) = COV(\varepsilon, z_*'\varepsilon) = COV(\varepsilon, \varepsilon_q) \tag{93}$$

(85) and (86) together imply

$$B \cdot v(\Delta) + v(\varepsilon) = B \cdot \Lambda \tag{94}$$

and, thus,

$$B_o v(\Delta) + v(\varepsilon^o) = B_o \Lambda \tag{95}$$

From (95) we get an expression for the market prices of systematic factor risk:

$$\Lambda = v(\Delta) + B_o^{-1} v(\varepsilon^o) \tag{96}$$

Using (92) and (93) we arrive at

$$\Lambda = b_q + B_o^{-1} COV(\varepsilon, \varepsilon_q) \tag{97}$$

Inserting (96) into (94) yields

$$Bv(\Delta) + BB_o^{-1} v(\varepsilon^o) = Bv(\Delta) + v(\varepsilon)$$

i.e.

$$v(\varepsilon) = BB_o^{-1} v(\varepsilon^o) \tag{98}$$

and, finally, by inserting (98) back into (96) one gets

$$\Lambda = b_q + B_o^{-1} BB_o^{-1} COV(\varepsilon^o, \varepsilon_q) \tag{99}$$

Looking at (98) we see that the no-arbitrage condition of the arbitrage pricing theory imposes a severe restriction on the residuals of the factor structure. Looking at(99) we see that the market prices of systematic factor risk are, in part, determined by the covariance risk of the idiosyncratic terms with the pricing portfolio; unless these covariances (which are like the betas in the CAPM) are zero this is a very unsatisfactory situation which is certainly not in the spirit of the arbitrage pricing theory where these unsystematic components are thought as unimportant as far as pricing is concerned.

LIST OF ASSUMPTIONS

(A1) There is an efficient portfolio (x^o, x) with $x \neq 0$.

(A2) No risk-neutral pricing, i.e. $E(P_1) \neq (1+r)P_o$.

(A3) The markets for risky assets are in equilibrium and the market portfolio x_M of all outstanding risky assets has a non-zero variance.

(A4) The covariance matrix C of risky assets is non-singular.

(A5) Assets are infinitely divisible, i.e. there can any non-negative real multiple of an asset be a part of a B/S-order.

(A6) Arbitration is effective, i.e. c(z) exists for each $z \in X_p$.

(A7) There are no spreads, i.e. $c(0) \geq 0$.

(A8) The cost functional is continuous with respect to every one-dimensional subspace of the portfolio space.

(A9) Standard free lunches are not possible.

(A10) There is a number $R(e^t)$ such that

$$E(D_{t+1}(x,.) + c_{t+1}(x,.)|e^t) = R(e^t)c_t(x,e^t)$$

for any portfolio x which is riskless over (t,t+1] conditional on e^t.

(A11) If x is a riskless portfolio over (t,t+1] and if $c_t(x,e^t) = 0$ holds, then $E(D_{t+1}(x,.) + c_{t+1}(x,.)|e^t) = 0$ must hold.

(A12) (A10) is true together with $R(e^t)$ being non-zero.

(A13) There is a positive number $R(e^t)$ such that

$$E(D_{t+1}(x,.) + c_{t+1}(x,.)|e^t) = R(e^t)c_t(x,e^t)$$

for any portfolio x which is riskless over (t,t+1].

INDEX OF FREQUENTLY USED SYMBOLS

The following

symbol	stands for	and is introduced on page number
c	cost functional	8,44
$\bar{c}$	cost function	44
C	covariance matrix of asset returns	8
$c_t(z,e^t)$	(minimal) net costs of executing portfolio change z at t given the history of events e^t	52
cov	covariance of two simple random variables	8
COV	covariance where at least one argument is a vector random variable	8
$D^t(.)$	stream of cash-payments for a portfolio held over (0,t]	62
$D_t(x,e^t)$	cash-flow received at t when e^t has happened and portfolio x has been held over (t-1,t]	52
$e^t = (e_o,e_1,\ldots,e_t)$	history of events $e_o,\ldots,e_t$ up to point in time t	51
$E(.)$	expected value of a (vector) random variable	9

G(.)	three-dimensional vector consisting of negative costs, expected return, negative variance of return of a portfolio	9
I(x,y)	set of possible ways to execute B/S-order (x,y)	44
$1_t = (0,\ldots,0,1,0,\ldots,0) \in \mathbb{R}^{T+1}$	spans the subset of deterministic processes	62
L	return operator	8
L^t	t-period return operator	62
μ	probability measure	77
N(.)	null space of a linear functional	83
N(.)	standardized normal distribution function	93
P_t	vector of ex-dividend asset prices observed at point in time t	7
q	state-dependent discount factor	78,79
$\hat{q}$	scarcity indicator of the price system	82
r	rate of return on the riskless asset	7
$(u_t \mid t \geq 0)$	consumption pattern	51
$U(x,e^t)$	set of consumption patterns derivable from portfolio x conditional on e^t	57
v,V	price functionals	61,63

var(.)	variance of a random variable	9
x or x_t	portfolio of (risky) assets held over period (t-1,t]	7
X	return space	8
$\overline{X}$	portfolio cone	43
X_p	portfolio space	7,44
Y	space of discrete time stochastic processes over [0,T]	61
z_t	vector of portfolio changes to be executed at t	52
$\oplus$	direct sum of real linear spaces	18
[.]	real linear subspace spanned by ·	18

REFERENCES

BACHMAN, G./NARICI, L., Functional Analysis, New York - London 1966

BEJA, A., The structure of the cost of capital under uncertainty, REVIEW OF ECONOMIC STUDIES 38 (1971), 359-368

BLACK, F., Capital market equilibrium with restricted borrowing, JOURNAL OF BUSINESS 44 (1972), 444-455

BLACK, F./SCHOLES,M., The pricing of options and corporate liabilities, JOURNAL OF POLITICAL ECONOMY 81 (1973), 637-659

BRENNAN, M.J., The pricing of contingent claims in discrete time models, JOURNAL OF FINANCE 34 (1979), 53-68

BRITO, N.O., Marketability restrictions and the valuation of capital assets under uncertainty, JOURNAL OF FINANCE 32 (1977), 1109-1123

CHAMBERLAIN, G./ ROTHSCHILD, M., Arbitrage, factor structures, and mean-variance analysis on large asset markets, ECONOMETRICA 51 (1983), 1281-1304

COX, J.C./INGERSOLL, J.E./ ROSS, S., The relation between forward prices and futures prices, JOURNAL OF FINANCIAL ECONOMICS 9 (1981), 321-346

COX, J.C./ ROSS, S./ RUBINSTEIN, M., Option pricing: a simplified approach, JOURNAL OF FINANCIAL ECONOMICS 7 (1979), 229-263

De ANGELO, H., Competition and unanimity, AMERICAN ECONOMIC REVIEW 71 (1981), 18-27

FELLER, W., An Introduction to Probability Theory and Its Applications, Vol. II, 2nd ed., New York - London - Sydney 1971

FRANKE, G., On tests of the arbitrage pricing theory, OR SPEKTRUM 6 (1984), 109-117

GARMAN, M.B./OHLSON, J.A., Valuation of risky assets in arbitrage-free economies with transaction costs, JOURNAL OF FINANCIAL ECONOMICS 9 (1981), 271-280

HARRISON, J.M./KREPS, D.M., Martingales and arbitrage in multiperiod securities markets, JOURNAL OF ECONOMIC THEORY 20 (1979), 381-408

HARRISON, J.M./ PLISKA, S., Martingales and stochastic integrals in the theory of continuous trading, STOCHASTIC PROCESSES AND THEIR APPLICATIONS 11 (1981), 215-260

-- / -- A stochastic calculus model of continuous trading: complete markets, STOCHASTIC PROCESSES AND THEIR APPLICATIONS 15 (1983), 313-316

HUBERMAN, G., A simple approach to arbitrage pricing theory, JOURNAL OF ECONOMIC THEORY 28 (1982), 183-191

JEVONS, W.S., The Theory of Political Economy, London 1871

KEYNES, J.M., A Tract on Monetary Reform, London 1923

LINTNER, J., Security prices, risk, and maximal gains from diversification, JOURNAL OF FINANCE 20 (1965), 587--615

-- Bankruptcy risk, market segmentation, and optimal capital structure, in: I. FRIEND/ J.L. BICKSLER (eds.), Risk and Return in Finance, Vol. II, Cambridge (Mass.) 1977, 1-128

MAYERS, D., Nonmarketable assets and capital market equilibrium under uncertainty, in: M.C. JENSEN (ed.), Studies in the Theory of Capital Markets, New York - Washington - London 1972, 223-248

MERTON, R.C., An intertemporal capital asset pricing model, ECONOMETRICA 41 (1973a), 867-887

-- Theory of rational option pricing, BELL JOURNAL OF ECONOMICS AND MANAGEMENT SCIENCE 4 (1973b), 141-183

MODIGLIANI, F./ MILLER, M.H., The cost of capital, corporation finance, and the theory of investment, AMERICAN ECONOMIC REVIEW 48 (1958), 261-297

MOSSIN, J., Equilibrium in a capital asset market, ECONOMETRICA 34 (1964), 768-783

MUNN, G.C., Encyclopedia of Banking and Finance, 8th edition, revised and expanded by F.L. GARCIA, Boston 1983

NEVEU, J., Mathematische Grundlagen der Wahrscheinlichkeitstheorie, München und Wien 1969

ROLL, R., A critique of the asset pricing theory's tests - Part I: On past and potential testability of the theory, JOURNAL OF FINANCIAL ECONOMICS 4 (1977), 129-176

--, ROSS, S.A., An empirical investigation of the arbitrage pricing theory, JOURNAL OF FINANCE 35 (1980), 1073-1101

ROSS, S.A., The arbitrage theory of capital asset pricing, JOURNAL OF ECONOMIC THEORY 13 (1976), 341-360

-- Risk, return and arbitrage, in: I. FRIEND/ J.L. BICKSLER (eds.), Risk and Return in Finance, Cambridge (Mass.) 1977, Vol. I, 189-218

-- A simple approach to the valuation of risky streams, JOURNAL OF BUSINESS 51 (1978), 453-475

RUBINSTEIN, M.E., Corporate financial policy in segmented securities markets, JOURNAL OF FINANCIAL AND QUANTITATIVE ANALYSIS 8 (1973), 749-761

-- The valuation of uncertain income streams and the pricing of options, BELL JORUNAL OF ECONOMICS AND MANAGEMENT SCIENCE 7 (1976), 407-425

RUDIN, W., Functional Analysis, New York 1973

SCHAEFER, H.H., Topological Vector Spaces, third printing corrected, New York - Heidelberg - Berlin, 1971

SHARPE, W.F., Capital asset prices: a theory of market equilibrium under conditions of risk, JOURNAL OF FINANCE 19 (1964), 425-442

STOLL, H.R., The relationship between put and call option prices, JOURNAL OF FINANCE 24 (1969), 801-824

WILHELM, J., Arbitrage, transaction costs, and the structure of asset returns, in: H. GÖPPL/ R.HENN (eds.), Geld, Banken und Versicherungen 1982/Band I, Karlsruhe 1983, 651-666

-- A consistent model for the pricing of derivative assets in a discrete time framework, in: G. BAMBERG/ K. SPREMANN (eds.), Risk and Capital, Berlin et al. 1984, 122-138

Vol. 213: Aspiration Levels in Bargaining and Economic Decision Making. Proceedings, 1982. Edited by R. Tietz. VIII, 406 pages. 1983.

Vol. 214: M. Faber, H. Niemes und G. Stephan, Entropie, Umweltschutz und Rohstoffverbrauch. IX, 181 Seiten. 1983.

Vol. 215: Semi-Infinite Programming and Applications. Proceedings, 1981. Edited by A. V. Fiacco and K. O. Kortanek. XI, 322 pages. 1983.

Vol. 216: H. H. Müller, Fiscal Policies in a General Equilibrium Model with Persistent Unemployment. VI, 92 pages. 1983.

Vol. 217: Ch. Grootaert, The Relation Between Final Demand and Income Distribution. XIV, 105 pages. 1983.

Vol. 218: P. van Loon, A Dynamic Theory of the Firm: Production, Finance and Investment. VII, 191 pages. 1983.

Vol. 219: E. van Damme, Refinements of the Nash Equilibrium Concept. VI, 151 pages. 1983.

Vol. 220: M. Aoki, Notes on Economic Time Series Analysis: System Theoretic Perspectives. IX, 249 pages. 1983.

Vol. 221: S. Nakamura, An Inter-Industry Translog Model of Prices and Technical Change for the West German Economy. XIV, 290 pages. 1984.

Vol. 222: P. Meier, Energy Systems Analysis for Developing Countries. VI, 344 pages. 1984.

Vol. 223: W. Trockel, Market Demand. VIII, 205 pages. 1984.

Vol. 224: M. Kiy, Ein disaggregiertes Prognosesystem für die Bundesrepublik Deutschland. XVIII, 276 Seiten. 1984.

Vol. 225: T. R. von Ungern-Sternberg, Zur Analyse von Märkten mit unvollständiger Nachfragerinformation. IX, 125 Seiten. 1984

Vol. 226: Selected Topics in Operations Research and Mathematical Economics. Proceedings, 1983. Edited by G. Hammer and D. Pallaschke. IX, 478 pages. 1984.

Vol. 227: Risk and Capital. Proceedings, 1983. Edited by G. Bamberg and K. Spremann. VII, 306 pages. 1984.

Vol. 228: Nonlinear Models of Fluctuating Growth. Proceedings, 1983. Edited by R. M. Goodwin, M. Krüger and A. Vercelli. XVII, 277 pages. 1984.

Vol. 229: Interactive Decision Analysis. Proceedings, 1983. Edited by M. Grauer and A. P. Wierzbicki. VIII, 269 pages. 1984.

Vol. 230: Macro-Economic Planning with Conflicting Goals. Proceedings, 1982. Edited by M. Despontin, P. Nijkamp and J. Spronk. VI, 297 pages. 1984.

Vol. 231: G. F. Newell, The M/M/∞ Service System with Ranked Servers in Heavy Traffic. XI, 126 pages. 1984.

Vol. 232: L. Bauwens, Bayesian Full Information Analysis of Simultaneous Equation Models Using Integration by Monte Carlo. VI, 114 pages. 1984.

Vol. 233: G. Wagenhals, The World Copper Market. XI, 190 pages. 1984.

Vol. 234: B. C. Eaves, A Course in Triangulations for Solving Equations with Deformations. III, 302 pages. 1984.

Vol. 235: Stochastic Models in Reliability Theory. Proceedings, 1984. Edited by S. Osaki and Y. Hatoyama. VII, 212 pages. 1984.

Vol. 236: G. Gandolfo, P.C. Padoan, A Disequilibrium Model of Real and Financial Accumulation in an Open Economy. VI, 172 pages. 1984.

Vol. 237: Misspecification Analysis. Proceedings, 1983. Edited by T. K. Dijkstra. V, 129 pages. 1984.

Vol. 238: W. Domschke, A. Drexl, Location and Layout Planning. IV, 134 pages. 1985.

Vol. 239: Microeconomic Models of Housing Markets. Edited b K. Stahl. VII, 197 pages. 1985.

Vol. 240: Contributions to Operations Research. Proceedings, 1984 Edited by K. Neumann and D. Pallaschke. V, 190 pages. 1985.

Vol. 241: U. Wittmann, Das Konzept rationaler Preiserwartunger XI, 310 Seiten. 1985.

Vol. 242: Decision Making with Multiple Objectives. Proceedings 1984. Edited by Y. Y. Haimes and V. Chankong. XI, 571 pages. 1985

Vol. 243: Integer Programming and Related Areas. A Classifie Bibliography 1981–1984. Edited by R. von Randow. XX, 386 pages 1985.

Vol. 244: Advances in Equilibrium Theory. Proceedings, 1984. Edite by C. D. Aliprantis, O. Burkinshaw and N. J. Rothman. II, 235 pages 1985.

Vol. 245: J. E. M. Wilhelm, Arbitrage Theory. VII, 114 pages. 1985

GPSR Compliance

The European Union's (EU) General Product Safety Regulation (GPSR) is a set of rules that requires consumer products to be safe and our obligations to ensure this.

If you have any concerns about our products, you can contact us on ProductSafety@springernature.com

In case Publisher is established outside the EU, the EU authorized representative is:

Springer Nature Customer Service Center GmbH
Europaplatz 3
69115 Heidelberg, Germany

Batch number: 10844675

Printed by Printforce, the Netherlands